Umpteen Pockets

Umpteen Pockets

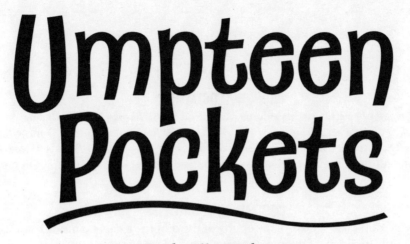

new and collected poems
for children

Adrian Mitchell

illustrated by Tony Ross

ORCHARD BOOKS

Orchard Books and Adrian Mitchell acknowledge
with thanks the Financial Assistance of the
Arts Council England, London.

ACKNOWLEDGEMENTS

Umpteen Pockets contains poems published in *All Shook Up* (Bloodaxe),
Blue Coffee (Bloodaxe), *Gynormous!* (Orion), *Nobody Rides The Unicorn* (Doubleday),
The Snow Queen (Oberon), *The Orchard Book of Poems*, *With Love*, *A Poem A Day*, *Zoo of
Dreams* and all the poems from *Balloon Lagoon* and *Daft as a Doughnut* (all Orchard).

GOOD LUCK, TEACHERS!

Please don't use these poems or any of my other work in exams or tests.
But I'm happy if people choose to read them aloud, learn them,
sing, dance or act them in or out of school.

ORCHARD BOOKS
338 Euston Road, London NW1 3BH
Orchard Books Australia
Level 17/207 Kent Street, Sydney, NSW 2000

First published in 2009 by Orchard Books
ISBN 978 1 40830 363 4

Umpteen Pockets text © Adrian Mitchell 2009
Balloon Lagoon text © Adrian Mitchell 1997
Daft as a Doughnut text © Adrian Mitchell 2004
Illustrations © Tony Ross 1997/2004/2009

The rights of Adrian Mitchell to be identified as the author of this work and of Tony Ross
to be identified as the illustrator of this work have been asserted by them in accordance
with the Copyrights, Designs and Patents Act, 1988.

A CIP catalogue record for this book is available from the British Library.

1 3 5 7 9 10 8 6 4 2

Printed in Great Britain

Orchard Books is a division of Hachette Children's Book,
an Hachette UK company.

www.orchardbooks.co.uk
www.hachette.co.uk

To my wife Celia
to my children and grand-children
to my nieces and nephews and their children
to my Mother and Father
to my animals
to all the children and teachers
who have made poetry with me

to the writers who delighted me most when I was a child:
Hans Christian Andersen, Anon, F. Anstey, M. E. Atkinson,
R. M. Ballantyne, Helen Bannerman, J. M. Barrie, R. D. Blackmore,
William Blake, Robert Browning, Jean de Brunhoff, John Buchan, John Bunyan,
Edgar Rice Burroughs, Lewis Carroll, G. K. Chesterton, Leslie Charteris,
Richmal Crompton, Daniel Defoe, Walter de la Mare, Charles Dickens,
Arthur Conan Doyle, Wanda Gag, H. L. Gee, Kenneth Grahame,
the Brothers Grimm, Gunby Hadath, H. Rider Haggard, Richard Jefferies,
Captain W. E. Johns, Erich Kastner, John Keats, Rudyard Kipling, Andrew Lang,
Stephen Leacock, Edward Lear, Hugh Lofting, Andre Maurois, Arthur Mee,
A. A. Milne, Edith Nesbit, George Orwell, Beatrix Potter, Arthur Ransome,
Dean Swift, Robert Louis Stevenson, Alfred Lord Tennyson, Katherine Tozer,
Mark Twain, Jules Verne, H. G. Wells, Percy F. Westerman, T. H. White,
Walt Whitman, P. G. Wodehouse and Johann D. Wyss, as well as the makers of
*Chicks' Own, The Dandy, The Beano, The Rover, The Hotspur, The Wag's Handbook,
The Boy's Own Paper, Punch, Batman, Superman, Classic Comics* and *Green Lantern*

to all those who work as writers, illustrators, publishers, booksellers,
librarians and parents, to bring children exciting and beautiful books

to you

Adrian Mitchell

ADRIAN MITCHELL
1932 — 2008

Like many wonderful writers before him,
Adrian Mitchell knew in his heart and in his pen that to write
for children was just as important (he would have said MORE
IMPORTANT!) as writing for grown-ups. Anyone lucky enough to
have attended one of Adrian's poetry gigs for young people would
certainly have laughed and clapped, probably danced, maybe gone
invisible and even have learned to fly — and all that before the
interval! Adrian had the deep silliness of the deadly serious. He loved
peace and children and animals, food and drink, his wife Celia, his
mum and dad, his friends, our beautiful planet, and every musician
from Louis Armstrong to The Beatles. And everyone who
encountered Adrian Mitchell through his poetry loved him.

When Adrian Mitchell died, not so long ago, all those people were
terribly sad. But I think, today, Adrian would not want us to be sad.
He would want us all to dive into this totally brilliant New and
Collected Poems for Children and have the BEST time. Adrian would
want every single reader to try on the coat with Umpteen Pockets and
see what she or he could find there. He'd want his readers to run
breathlessly in the wake of Daisy the Dog of Peace; to listen to the
Song of Merlin (as he turns sadly into an owl) and to Beatrix Potter's
Song, so poignantly relevant to our modern environmental problems.
And there is more... and more... and MORE!

When I read Adrian Mitchell's poems on the pages of this fantastic book, I can hear his voice and rhythms in my head — and I think this will be true for every young reader, even if they never heard Adrian perform. If you read these poems, I promise you will hear Adrian Mitchell's exuberant voice-music, his anger at war and injustice, his compassion for the hurt, his love and celebration of all things bright and beautiful. You'll hear his feet tapping along the lines and his friendly dog bounding along beside him. And you'll hear a secret and know it to be true... that good poets don't really die, they live on in their poems. So here's the gorgeous, human, funny, passionate, superb children's poet, Adrian Mitchell — LARGER than life!

Carol Ann Duffy
Poet Laureate

This is a kaleidoscope of poems, full of fantasy, foot-tapping and fun.
Here we can visit the Planet Fluff, Rainbow Woods, and Big Dog river. We can meet a chocolate-coloured calf, the King of Zing, the Czar of Zoom, Postman Horse and a kitten called Moonlight.
But what shall we eat? Runny Hunny of course.
"Slurp, slurp, slurp, then give a sweet burp."
It's all here in Adrian's last and long-lasting and wonder-making book of poems.

Michael Rosen

Adrian Mitchell was the greatest Word Magician and Poem Juggler! He was the Supreme Commander of the Happy Alphabet and wrote poems that tasted better than doughnuts and that were as bright as stars. It's wonderful to have this very special collection of his work.

Brian Patten

UMPTEEN POCKETS

CONTENTS

Umpteen Scenery

Adrian Mitchell

The Coat with Umpteen Pockets

It was the dawn of my Umpteenth Birthday.
I followed Daisy Dog over the scruffy lawn
Then stopped and laughed as I saw
Swinging on a silver hanger
From a branch of our good old Apple Tree –
The Coat with Umpteen Pockets.

Of course I wondered who left it for me,
But I didn't want to ask
Wanting to keep wondering
Not wanting to break the spell
I simply said Thank you Apple Tree
And took down the Coat with Umpteen Pockets.

The coat fitted me like a glove
If a glove was a coat
You could wear in any kind of weather
I wanted to sing
It was like sprouting wings
In my coat tough as leather
But light as a feather
My Coat with Umpteen Pockets.

Umpteen Pockets

Umpteen pockets of different sizes and shapes
And colours I'd never seen
Now each pocket has a name and also a number
From the square root of Minus Zero up to Umpteen.

I'll put on my Umpteenth Birthday Coat
And the people – I shall show 'em
That every one of the Umpteen Pockets
Is the Home of a Poem
In my Coat of Umpteen Pockets.

EASY INSTRUCTIONS FOR THE WEARER
OF THE COAT WITH UMPTEEN POCKETS

It's a simple kind of mystery
to operate
a Coat of Umpteen Pockets.

The Coat comes with a Helpful Booklet
of Easy Instructions,
a green Booklet
printed on the leaves of a Koolibah tree.

Adrian Mitchell

But on the very day I found the Coat
I made the shortsighted mistake
of placing my Spectacles
in the pocket marked Sausages.

Seeing a little blurrily
I then stashed my Helpful Booklet away
in a pocket marked in scarlet letters:

One minute later
I felt a tremor in that compartment
and out belched smoke and flames
and the burning remains
of my Helpless Booklet.

Only one thing for it –
thanks to my powerful spectacles
I found the Mermaid Pocket
(which is full of salt water
in case I ever catch a Mermaid.

Umpteen Pockets

It has a transparent panel on the outside
and contains eels, living seaweed,
anemones, starfish and seahorses
and is secured by a waterproof zip.)

I stuffed the Booklet
into the Mermaid Pocket –
there was a wild cloud of steam
and the fire was out.

But my Helpful Booklet
was all bedraggled
its pages in pieces
its words all woebegone.

The Instructions were
all smeared and smudged
and scrappy and hard to understand –
even when seen through
my powerful Sausages (I mean Spectacles).

Howsumever, I'll try to tell you about
all of the Umpteen Coat Guidelines which survive.

The Helpful Booklet comes with this Warning:
"Never wear the Coat with Umpteen Pockets
unless you want to write a poem
or read a poem or recite a poem
or sing a poem or fly a poem…"

(There are a few leaves missing at this point.
Then the Booklet continues.)

"Outdoors, you should wear your Coat with Umpteen Pockets
    with Numblejum Boots and a Gillydrop Hat.
The Umpteen Pockets
    contain a jillion or a zillion Secrets.
There are so many pockets in your Coat
    that you may decide, one day,
    to count them all.

This endeavour could take
    until the end of your days.
But, should you decide
    to count the Pockets –
    please use the following
    Simple Guide to Counting in Umpteens."

Numpty Counting

(A simple guide to counting in Umpteens)

APHRUMPTEEN

BUMPTEEN

CHUMPTEEN

DUMPTEEN

EXUMPTEEN

FRUMPTEEN

GRUMPTEEN

HUMPTEEN

INUMPTEEN

JUMPTEEN

KUMPTEEN

LUMPTEEN

MUMPTEEN
NUMPTEEN
OZUMPTEEN
PLUMPTEEN

QUOMPTEEN
RUMPTEEN
STUMPTEEN
THUMPTEEN

UMPTEEN
VAMPTEEN
WUMPTEEN
XIMPTEEN

YUMPA-YUMPA-YUMPTEEN

ZUMP-ZUMP-APHRUMPTEEN!!!

The Helpful Booklet

(At this point there is a leaf missing,
but the Booklet continues like this…)

"…many many many many pockets –
multi-coloured pockets
inside and outside.

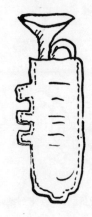

Some are pockets within pockets
with pockets within them.
Some are zipped or buttoned
or padlocked or clipped like purses.

Transparent pockets you can look into,
or look out of for that matter.

Heart-shaped pockets
Broken heart-shaped pockets
Stained glass pockets
and expandable pockets

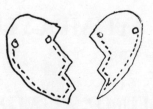

Book pockets
A pocket for a trumpet
A drumkit pocket
so anyone can thump it

A clock pocket
to count each minute
A Jacket pocket
with a jacket folded in it

Firework pockets
with rockets
Electric pockets
with sockets

Secret pockets
Big pockets
Cunning disguise
and wig pockets

A pocket for losing
called Lucy Lockett
A fake raccoonskin hat one
called Davy Crockett

Umpteen Pockets

A fatherly pocket
with crumbs for robins on the lawn
A motherly pocket
with poppies glowing in the corn

A dictionary pocket
full of wonderful words
A rescue cage pocket
for injured animals and birds

A Country pocket
with daisy-bright turf
A Seaside pocket
with bumping white surf

A Lost and Found pocket
to end every search
A Wildwood pocket
for a silver birch

Adrian Mitchell

Drop your recipes
into the Menu Slot
and your meal will appear there
piping hot

In your Polar Bear pocket
ice creams are found
and unlimited snowballs
all the year round

There are pockets
for toffee and chocolate bars
and a Universe pocket
full of planets and stars

A dark pocket for an Owl
and an Icicle Pump
and a Memories pocket
and a Rubbish Dump

There's a Pancake Pocket
And a paper Moonshade
A Toolpocket with wheelbarrow,
bucket and spade

A clockwork pocket
Just to wind you up
And a petting pocket
with a kitten and a pup.

Oodles of noodles..."

Adrian Mitchell

(At this point, about foggleteen pages seem to be missing. There are only two leaves left. The first one says:)

"Some poems come from a pocket full of Mud
Some do come from a pocket full of Blood
Some come from pockets which have no name
or pockets with no number, it's all the same –
so long as the poems you sing are true –
be kind to them and they'll be good to you."

*(And the last leaf is all burned or blurred away
except for these words:)*

"...don't forget your Conscience Pockets.
You have two. One is your

INBOX CONSCIENCE

This is where you put
all the bad things in the world you worry about
like wars and gangs and famine and floods.
In this pocket lives a Dragon
who is the size of a mouse.
Look after him.

The other is your

OUTBOX CONSCIENCE

This is where you put
all the bad things you have done
and all the good things you haven't done.

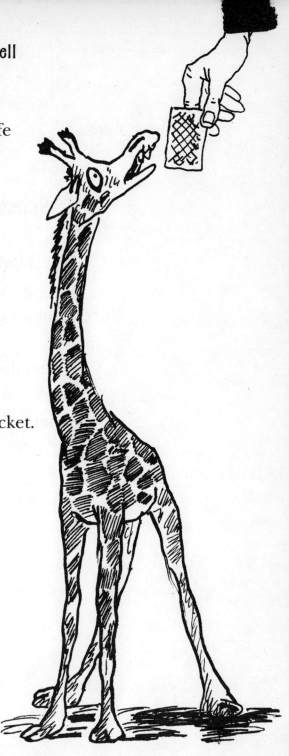

In this pocket lives a sensible Giraffe
who leans out
and licks your cheek
when you need affection.
She will look after you.

The Dragon and the Giraffe
in these two pockets
have to be fed.
Get your Dragon treats
and Giraffe wafers
from the Wild Animal Pet Shop Pocket.

Give your Dragon and Giraffe
plenty of exercise.
Let them out every day
to play with each other..."

*(The end of the Helpful Handbook
to the Coat of Umpteen Pockets.)*

Scottish Shoulders

When I was about nine or ten
a nurse said to me
Oh you've got Scottish shoulders.

So the Umpteen Coat
may be heavy
But my Scottish shoulders

swing it along
to a happy-go-lucky tune.

Magical Pockets

Took a Job

Took a job as the ghost of a pirate
In a castle owned by a vampire
But I scared myself so much that overnight
My teeth fell out and my hair turned white
And I had to take a job as a liar and a grandpa.

A Dog called Sorry

A dog called Sorry
A cat called Thank You
A baby called Maybe
A man called No
A woman called Yes
A boy called Forest
A girl called Lake

lived in the great city of Suppose
on the island of July
lived on the far island of October.

Adrian Mitchell

The Flying Pool

I'd like a silver door that leads
To a corridor of dreams that slopes down gradually at first
Then steeper and steeper, you can hardly keep your feet,
Then steeper, your feet slip back from under you,
Then vertical and you round a corner falling
And find yourself high in a deep deep windowless room
Gliding in circles and below you your friends
Their arms outstretched in ecstasy

As they circle and spin

And rise and fall

Among the swirling currents

Of the air of our Flying Pool.

Merlin's Song

*(After watching a terrible battle, Merlin the Magician
decided to live for the rest of his life as an owl in a wood.)*

I have walked through the valley of slate
And the rain was blue
I have seen the sky like a hunter's net
Deepest darkest blue
I have seen the bit tight in the horse's teeth
And the bit was blue
I have heard swords sing on the battlefield
And the swords were blue
I have seen the eyes of my dead foe
They were round as the world and blue
I have seen the face of my friend in the dawn
On the sheep-shorn grass – his face was blue

Adrian Mitchell

Blue grave
Blue gravel on a grave
Blue flowers on the gravel on a grave

And I shall wake in the blue night
And sleep in the blue day
And I will live my own blue life
In the blue tree in the blue tree

And my food shall be blue
And my wine shall be blue
And my mind shall be filled
With nothing but blue

blue blue   blue blue   blue blue

The Backwards Birthday Curse

On a good day I'm a pretty wicked Wizard
On a good day I'm bad
I'm about as pleasant as the gizzard of a lizard
Don't make me mad
On a good day I'm a pretty wicked Wizard
And your good day will be a sad day
On a good day I'm as awful as a blizzard –
You caught me on a Bad Day!

I put you under my favourite spell – they don't come any worse –
Yes – it's the terrifying Backwards Birthday Curse.

It's December now and you're Twenty-One.
Now listen closely, this'll be fun.
In January you'll be Twenty, strange to say.
In February you'll be Nineteen
And Eighteen in March, do you see what I mean?
Seventeen in April, Sixteen in May,
Fifteen in June, Fourteen in July,
You're getting younger, day by day,
Watch how quickly the months fly by.

Adrian Mitchell

Thirteen in August, Twelve in September,
Eleven in November, Ten in December.
Another January and you'll be Nine,
Gradually gradually shrinking away.
Eight in February, Seven in March,
Six in April and Five in May,
Four in June and Three in July,
Two in August, One in September,
But in October, that's best of all,
You'll be Nought, you'll be Zero and Nothing at all.

On a good day I'm a pretty wicked Wizard
And your good day will be a sad day
On a good day I'm as awful as a blizzard –
You caught me on a Bad Day!

New Lamps For Old

(*from* Aladdin)

Shadows are growing longer…
Sky is silvery, dark blue and brown.
Children are turning sleepy.
The Sun is weary, his golden head is heavy
And he feels like laying it down.

And there's darkness falling on the pavement,
Darkness falling on the Square.
Down the little alleys, on the Royal Palace,
Darkness falling everywhere.

But a strange man's walking into our street
And he stands below my window in the night.
And he looks up at me and he whispers: Can't you see?
I've brought you a present – it's a beautiful new light.

Adrian Mitchell

New lamps for old! New lamps for old!
Let's illuminate this grimy gloomy ghostly town.
New lamps for old! New lamps for old!
It's an offer that you can't turn down.
Swap that rusty lantern for an every-shining light!
Chase away the monsters of the night!
      New lamps for old!

Anybody there? Anybody listening?
See my brand-new shining lamps, see them glistening
Brighter than the Morning in her gown of gold –
      New lamps for old! New lamps for old!

Unicorn Horn

Here's how it is:

Find yourself a fiery dragonfly.
Tempt her, with a smear of honey,
to bite a small crater in the middle of your forehead.
Cover the crater with a silver birch leaf.
Next you must collect a mermaid's tear
at midnight by moonlight on midsummer's eve.
There's a kind of music makes a mermaid cry –
like the song of a white whale maybe
or the song of the nightingale maybe
like the song of a whirlpool under a waterfall.

So play your mermaid the waterfall music
and she will weep – a single tear.
Before the tear can fall into the grass
it will have turned into a pearly seed.

Now take that pearl,
plant it in your dragonfly crater.
Cover it over with a disc of mud
from the hoof of an African hippo.

Seven nights later you will feel
more than a tickle but less than a burn
as the golden bud of a horn bursts out
of your happy foreheadfrom into the air.

Well, how long it'll grow and how long that takes
depends upon the clarity and depth of your dreams.
As you walk around with your unicorn's horn
you may be mocked for it, feared for it, loved for it –
but your life will always be touched by magic.

Budapest Fluff

on the shining tiles
of swimming pool steps
head-size portions
of this ghostly stuff
materialise

large lumps of underbed fluff
or so it seems

But no, the trained botanist points out,
Budapest has trees which release
groups of froth or fluff
something to do with reproduction
a sort of aerial treespawn

Adrian Mitchell

Apparently floating pointlessly
in clumps and flossles
it bowls along the highways fooling motorists
rolls across the football pitch
to enter the goalie's open mouth
The fluff, the fluff –
it bloweth where it listeth
and it listeth more or less everywhere

thousands of fluffballs falling gracefully
out of the wide blue sky
each little cloud
containing one bright white seed

aliens from the Planet Fluff
maybe maybe

People Packets

Beatrix Potter's Song

When I was very small,
London was very big.
My only friends were a wooden doll
And a grimy little cotton pig.

When I was very small,
Grown-ups were enormous.
They never noticed me at all –
A timid little dormouse.

But whenever summertime came around
We took a magical ride
In a train that puffed all the way up to Scotland
And its windy, friendly-smelling countryside.

Umpteen Pockets

Eagles and mountains
And rocky little rivers,
The fox on the hill
And the frogs by the lake,

Rabbits and hedgehogs
And tabby-cats and squirrels –
They were my friends
And they danced for my sake.

Deer in the forest
And ducklings in the farmyard,
The sheepdog who smiled
And the shy little snake,

All of the creatures,
The wild ones, the tame ones –
They were my friends
And they sang for my sake.

Adrian Mitchell

I remember every stone
And the scent of the heather
And the growling of the thunder
And the shadows of the trees.
I remember the bats
As they flitted round the farmyard
And the strange deep music
Of the summer breeze.

Deer in the forest
And ducklings in the farmyard,
The sheepdog who smiled
And the shy little snake.

All of the creatures,
The wild ones, the tame ones,
They were my friends
And they sang for my sake.

My Father and Mother
or How I Began to Hate War

My father was small and quiet, with a brown face
And lines of laughter round his eyes
And wildly sprouting Scottish eyebrows.
Everybody called my father Jock.
In 1914 he joined the army.
He fought for four years in the mud of the trenches.

Nearly all his friends were killed in that war.
He told me about one friend of his
Who suddenly, in the lull between bombardments,
Fell on all fours, howled like an animal,
And was never cured.
My father was a small and quiet man.

My mother was called Kay.
She had blue eyes and a comical nose
And a doll called Beauty.
And she had two older brothers
Called Sydney and Stanley.
Sydney was dark and Stanley was fair

And they used to pull my mother's long gold plaits –
And she loved them very dearly.

In 1914 Sydney joined the army
And was killed within days.
Next year Stanley went to the war
To take revenge for his brother.
But Stanley was killed as well.

In 1918 my father came home
With a sword and a kilt and shrapnel in his arm
And Jock and Kay met and fell in love
At the Presbyterian Badminton Club.

And in good time they had two sons
And one of us was dark and one was fair.
And I think, in a way, my brother James and I
Came here to take the place of Sydney and Stanley –
My mother's two beloved brothers.

And when I think about war I remember
How when Remembrance Day came round each year,
My mother always war two poppies.

Rainbow Woods

I was nearly seven when War broke out.
My brother James and I were evacuated
To Combe Down, a village of bright stone
On the hill above the city of Bath.
My friends and I were always being chased
Out of farmland and parkland and private estates.
Boys Keep Out. Trespassers Will Be Executed.
Till we found a free place, Rainbow Woods.

Rainbow Woods, as bright as a paint-box,
Packed with steep hills and curving pathways,
A switchback speedway
Buzzing with kids on bikes,
Scooting over the roots,
Whirring and whirling through the air
To crash-land in bushes.

Adrian Mitchell

Running kids, climbing kids,
Kids crawling under heaps of autumn leaves,
Kids with dogs and catapults
Totally ignored by the adult world.

Rainbow Woods
With a thousand trees
And a hundred hills.
Rainbow Woods
With its mysterious ruin
Like a palace for ghosts…

Putsborough Sands

At the seaside my brother and I took flight.
We leapt down the sand-dunes in giant strides
Like the god Mercury with wings on his heels
And we called this sandhill flying – Mercurying.

The wonderful freedom of limitless sand…
We constructed intricate systems of canals
To feed the enormous dams we built
Out of rocks and sand, dams that filled and filled
Till we could stand waist-deep in their waters.

The wonderful freedom – and safety too,
For our brown-faced father sat at the end
Of a distant rock fishing peacefully
While our mother dozed in her deckchair or read
Biographies with her blue eyes through blue spectacles.
We were free, we were safe, you could call it peace…

Peace was a banana milk-shake in a café.

Putsborough beach where I first fell in love.
I remember the moment. I was fourteen.

Adrian Mitchell

Her dark hair was flowing over her freckles.
She stood barefoot in her turquoise dress,
Then her brown arms swung
And the bat in her hand smashed the rounders ball
And also my heart, way into the distance.

And I loved her silently for four years
And wrote eight hundred midnight poems for her
Which I was ashamed to show to my dog…

My Small Green Geography Teacher

My first geography teacher had a hunched-up back
She was small and always wore a green cardigan
And she travelled with her missionary parents
Taking medicine and Jesus to the people of China.

Once we spent the whole of a May morning
Travelling in a wooden boat up the yellow waters
Of the great river called the Yangtse-Kiang,
Fishing with cormorants,
Walking barefoot through dusty villages
And lying in the bottom of our boat at night
Watching the moon as it floated by.

My small green geography teacher
Smiled at the people on the banks of the river
And the people of China smiled at us.

Beatle Day

Jenny bumped into the Beatles
On her Beatle Day.
If anyone asks her about it
This is what Jenny will say:

Oh yes, I bumped into the Beatles,
I was even younger than you.
They were the greatest group in the world,
They were making a film at the Zoo.

I'd seen all the lions and tigers
And a Keeper with a pet mouse,
Then I bumped into all four Beatles
Beside the Elephant House.

John gave a chimp a piggy-back.
Paul sang to a giraffe.
George fed a bun to a furry bear
And all Ringo did was laugh.

Umpteen Pockets

I made the Beatles all stand in a line
And took their photograph.
John winked, Paul grinned and George looked sad
But all Ringo did was laugh.

And then we sat down on the grass
Beside the Zoo Café.
The Beatles made up a song for me
Called Hey Jenny Hey!

John, Paul and George each gave me a kiss
And tickets to hear them play,
But Ringo gave me a jelly baby
And I've kept it to this day.

That night I took my Mum to hear
The wonderful Beatles play
And there I bumped into my boyfriend Bill
And I've kept him to this day.

When we watched the Beatles play their songs
They were full of fire and fun.
They jumped about and sang Twist And Shout
They were friends with everyone.

Well they never recorded that Jenny song
But I sing it anyway:
Hey Jenny, brighter than a penny,
Hey Jenny Hey!

That's how Jenny bumped into the Beatles
Down at the London Zoo.
If you don't think they're the best group in the world
Jenny will bump into you.

Gullible

My legs are getting shorter,
I told my daughter.
Know what? I reckoned
She believed me for a second.

I've Been Trying to Think

I don't think it's right to kill people

a man might strangle two schoolgirls
boys might burn a tramp to death
a wife might poison her husband's dinner
a pilot might bomb a city and
kill one hundred people in a night
it all seems wrong

I don't think it's right to kill animals either
but I eat some of them
chickens and fish and stuff

I don't think it's right for the sea to drown people
and earthquakes shouldn't bury families
in rocks and mud and broken houses
nor should volcanoes

as far as I know
the sea and the earth do not have consciences
but if they do

they maybe have their own ideas
of what is right and wrong

I am only a child
but I have always been very interested
in right and wrong
when I do something bad
I am usually sorry
straight away
sometimes it takes time
but I'm nearly always sorry in the end

when bad things are done to me
I fight back if I can
but usually bad things are done to me
by people who are bigger and stronger
I ask them to stop
they don't often stop
if you just ask them
they might stop if you scream
they might
but if you scream
you might be in very bad trouble

My Genius

My name is Linda.
I am a fourteen-year-old poet
in a huge class
in an enormous school
I don't know why

My desk is next to the desk
of Skruff, Boy Genius

Most of the kids
laugh at him
and call him Skruff
he looks through them

Teachers yell at him
Gangs try to pick on him
Come here, Skruff!!
he dodges them
But sometimes round to me
he gives me a smile
and it goes straight
to my heart

Adrian Mitchell

So I write poems for Skruff
not saying out loud
I love you
poems more like paper flowers

I give him a poem
He gives me a smile

I think maybe
Skruff hasn't got a home
Maybe he lives in the woods
with a white dog called Shadow

I daydream about him
I've started to write
whole books about him

SKRUFF is the first book
and it introduces him
and his white dog Shadow

Umpteen Pockets

ROUGH SKRUFF is the second
and it tells how
he outwits a gang
called the Badnecks

SKRUFF LOST is about him
(and Shadow) going on a journey
to find his Mum and Dad

SPOTLIGHT ON SKRUFF
is about him getting to be
a famous pianist like Jools Holland
(this one's a bit fantastic)

SKRUFF GONE is the last one
that I've done
and is about Skruff disappearing
this is a sad one

I have written all five books
and illustrated them
all ready for his birthday
on April 24th

The Clown is Dead

Children must learn that fairy tales are lies,
Faces are masks, and peace is out of reach.
I stare into the clown's unwinking eyes
Discovering the child they could not teach.

Though he rode out of childhood cheerfully
He left that forest for the open lands
In fear of other men. He could not see
If they held knives or flowers in their hands.

Seeing the animals, he learnt to speak
Solemnly to them, and at length remove
Their simple terrors; for if he was weak
In anything, it was not in his love.

* * *

Death came to him when he was young
And he stuck out his scarlet tongue.
He went to Death when he was old:
"Take me," he said, "it's turning cold."

The Bearded Lady and the Tattooed Man
Played cards inside his caravan.
We sat around his tousled bed,
Shivered with him till he was dead.

That was a quiet way to fade,
For him, who loved to sit astride
The high giraffe in the parade,
With blare and bang of brass and hide.

It was a quiet way to fall.
Into the ring he used to come
With a high tragic caterwaul –
And always fell upon his bum.

* * *

What was the colour of his mind?
It was a prism, casting lights,
Changing, revolving in the wind
Of roaring days and storming nights.

Our elephants of laughter strode
Across his earthy doubletalk.
He goaded them to a stampede
And shot them with a popping cork.

He met tired walkers every day.
They were ill with travelling.
His songs enchanted them to stay:
They learnt to sing.

What's left? A clown of empty cloth,
A crumpled rainbow on the floor
Of a black cupboard. The destroying moth
Nests in the shapeless hat he wore.

What remains with any man?
There is no answer.
In this circus no one can
Dance, but he was a dancer.

He had no children, but I would
Stand as his son, to keep his name
And watch his footsteps take the road
Of prancing beyond praise or blame.

The gentle unicorn has gone away.
The dodo, poker-faced and knockabout,
Saw that its tail was turning grey,
Ate up the door and waddled out.

In his good time he followed these
Moonstruck and happy monsters. All
His laughter has gone with him, and like these
He is extinct or mythical.

And he is fabulously still;
The greasepaint grin wiped off his face
By lightly sliding hands, until
The naked lips grin in its place.

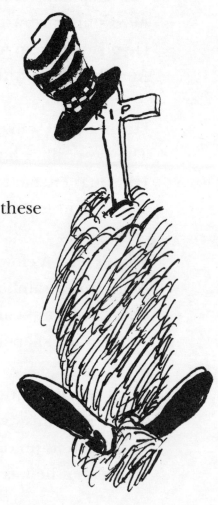

* * *

In his hands put an apple from a tree,
Bury him deep so no one can see,
For a dead man's smile tears the whole heart down.
The clown is dead. Long live the clown.

Adrian Mitchell

On Seeing the Queen in a Country Lane
On Her Return from a Visit to Dartmouth in 1998
by Adrian Mitchell the Shadow Poet Laureate

I thought we'd been held up for an accident
But that was not what the policemen meant
As they waved from the motorbikes they stood astride
For us to stop and wait by the roadside.

After a while came a black limousine
And then another. In it was the Queen.
I saw her sitting in the back. It's true.
She did not wave at us. Her hat was blue.

David and Goliath Rap

Once upon a time there was a terrible war –
Though no one ever told me what the war was for –
But the army of the Philistine was hot for a fight
And so was the army of the Israelite.

They shouted at each other, they hollered and cursed
But nobody wanted to charge in first
When a Philistine giant stepped from the front rank
With a ton of brass armour going clank clank clank.

He was eleven feet high and so was his spear.
He yelled: "My name's Goliath, and I've come here
To ask you to send me a man to fight –
Come on – feed me an Israelite."

But none of the Israelites fancied a tussle
With eleven foot of blood bone brass and muscle
Till a kid called David says: "I know about giants,
They can always be beaten by a little bit of science."

Adrian Mitchell

The King of Israel says: "Forget it, son,
He weighs ten ton, you'll be out in round one."
David says: "I can take him, OK?"
King Saul says: "Who are you, anyway?"

"I'm just a shepherd boy, but I guard my flock
With a wicked little sling that I load with rock.
Every one of the slings I've slung were aces –
I can hit a wolf's nose at a thousand paces.

"I smashed up a lion and demolished a bear
And I'll do just the same to that hulk over there."
David grinned and the King gave a sigh
And said: "You've got the guts, boy, give it a try."

David takes a staff and he goes to look
For five smooth pebbles from a nearby brook.
Then he calls out: "Goliath, you're in for a shock."
And Goliath replieth: "I'm ready to rock."

When Goliath sees David he cackles: "Little boy,
I'm going to shake you and break you like a baby's toy,
I'll crack your every bone from your skull to your toes
And I'll feed what's left to the jackals and crows."

Umpteen Pockets

All the Israelite army shudders with fear
When Goliath gives a roar and lifts his mighty spear
And the shadow of the giant falls cold on the land –
But David just smiles as he takes his stand.

And he takes one pebble and pops it in his sling
And he slings that sling in a circling ring
And he slings that sling and he lets go – now!
And there's a pebble sunk deep in Goliath's brow.

For a moment there's a look of terrible surprise
Which lights up both of that giant's eyes,
Then the lights go out and Goliath is dead
With his face in the dust and a stone in his head.

So that's a happy ending for old King Saul
And the army of Israel and most of all
For little David with his cunning sling –
And that shepherd boy grew up to be King.

But when Goliath's mother read the Palestine Post
And learned how her loving son gave up the ghost,
Her great tears flooded the wilderness
And the whole world shook at the grief of a giantess.

Miss Nightingale's Owl

1. THE ANIMAL HOSPITAL
In a wild, enormous garden
Two sisters were having a feast.
Flo and Parthe sat in their palace made of branches.
The big pine-cones were peaches.
The small pine-cones were tangerines.
The beech-nuts were strawberries
And the conkers were gooseberries.

It was a funeral feast.
Flo and Parthe had found a dead blue-tit.
They took it to their animal burying-ground.
Flo wrote this poem. She recited it over the grave:

> *Tomtitty bird! Why art thou dead?*
> *Thou who dost bear upon thy head*
> *A crown! But now thou art on thy death bed.*
> *My Tom Tit.*

Flo and Parthe spent every summer
In that wild, enormous garden.
They used a dusty little greenhouse
As an animal hospital.
They cared for sick and wounded
Dogs, cats, birds, beetles and worms.

2. FLO MEETS A BEAR

Years later, when Flo was almost grown up,
She was taken to lunch with Professor Buckland,
The animal expert.
Suddenly Bruno, his three-month-old bear, ambled in.
He climbed on the table and scoffed all the butter.
Professor Buckland put on his black cap and gown
And told Bruno off – but he stood on his hind legs
And growled and howled and shook his paws in the air.
Flo spoke to the bear, but the Professor warned her:
"He may be in a biting mood today."
"Don't worry," said Flo, "I'm going to hypnotise him."
And she spoke very softly to the bear
And she tickled his chest very gently
And the little bear began to yawn
And then he lay down
And in three minutes he was asleep and snoring.

3. FLO SAVES AN OWL
When she was a little older and taller
Flo wanted to travel round the world.
In Egypt she sailed up the river Nile
With two chameleons, who slept on her bed.

In Greece she adopted two tortoises,
Called Mr and Mrs Hill
And an enormous grasshopper named Plato.

One evening Flo was visiting
The famous Acropolis in Athens
When she saw a gang of children
Throwing stones at a ball of fluff.
It was a baby owl.
It had fallen out of its nest on one of the temple's pillars.

Flo saved the little owl.
She bought her from the children
For a few little coins
And named her Athena,
After the Greek goddess of Wisdom.

4. TRAINING A LITTLE OWL

At first Athena was angry with Flo.
She bit and kicked and swore in her cage.
But Flo tempted her out with a piece of meat.
She spoke very softly to the owlet
And she tickled her chest very gently
And the little owl began to yawn
And then she laid her silky head in Flo's lap
And in two minutes she was asleep and snoring.

Soon Athena was quite well behaved.
She ate her meals from Flo's hand.
They travelled together to Prague
Where Plato the grasshopper died
And then Athena ate him up –
So now Flo had two pets in one.
It was in Prague that a waiter saw Athena and shouted:
"Look, that's the bird all English ladies carry everywhere,
Because it tells them when they're going to die!"

5. ATHENA MAKES FRIENDS

When Flo arrived back home in England
She walked up through the wild, enormous garden,
In at the French windows
And sat down quietly on the sofa
Between her mother and Parthe.
They had talked for nearly half an hour
When Athena's head stuck out of her pocket.

Athena fluttered on to the table.
She gave a curtsey to Parthe
And a bow to Flo's mother.
Then she began to explore the house.

The little owl had a few special friends –
They were allowed to stroke her almost flat,
And hold her by her head,
And pull her tail,
And blow on her feathers.
She hated to be ignored.

She would sit on Flo's finger for her daily meal,
Opening her wings wide
As she swallowed little scraps of meat.
But she wasn't so good with strangers –
She could bite and scratch –
And she didn't trust children.

6. ATHENA'S IDEA OF FUN

Athena liked to spend her mornings,
In the library with Flo and Parthe.
When she was tired of hearing them read aloud,
She explored the shelves
Or played hide and seek behind the books.

If there was an armchair by the fire
Athena knew it had been put there for her.
She would stand in the middle of its seat,
Shut one of her eyes,
Draw up one leg and perch for an hour at a time.

Her favourite game was to knock over a vase of roses,
Steal the best rose, perch out of reach
And pick all the petals off the flower.

Athena enjoyed conversation.
She had five ways of talking.
A bark when she was naughty.
A crowing when she was proud.
A little purr – "twee twee" – when she was happy.
A grumble when she was cross.
A hoot when she was sad.

Her eyesight was wonderful.
She could see a fly from the far end of a long room,
Glide swiftly down and pounce on it.
One day she was dreaming on top of a bookshelf
When a mouse scuffled out.
Athena dropped like a stone
And swallowed the mouse – whiskers, tail and all.

7. FLO NURSES ATHENA

She was a healthy little owl.
But now and then she had a fit.
Then she would fall down on her side
And lie as if she'd been knocked out.

Umpteen Pockets

When this happened Flo wrapped her in a flannel
And talked to her beside the fire
And soon Athena would say: *"Twee, twee,"*
And tell Flo all her troubles.
Then she would burst out of the flannel
And hop about as if nothing had happened.

She was very brave indeed.
She would stand at an open window on tipclaw
Barking at a dog fifty times her size.
She was only once known to be scared.
That was when a friend brought round this present –
A china owl with great big eyes,
Lit from inside by a candle.

8. GOODBYE, ATHENA

Then the Crimean War broke out.
Miss Florence Nightingale – which was Flo's full name –
Was asked to take a team of nurses to the war.
But wars are too dangerous for little owls,
So when Flo took a ship to Turkey
She left Athena with her sister Parthe.
One day Athena had a fit and then lay still.
Parthe talked to her, stroked her and nursed her,
But it was no good.

Far away in Scutari,
Florence Nightingale became the most famous nurse in history.
The wounded soldiers called her "The Lady With The Lamp".
Their hospital was like a terrible nightmare,
But Florence worked bravely, day and night.
She comforted the men and cured them when she could.

Umpteen Pockets

Miss Nightingale went back to England for a short rest.
She walked with Parthe in the wild, enormous garden.
Parthe told Flo how she'd wrapped the cold Athena in her flannel
And buried her by the hollow oak-tree.
Flo had seen hundreds of soldiers die
But she had a tear for the little owl.
"Poor little Beastie," she said.

The sisters walked together under peaceful trees,
Till they came to their palace made of branches
And they talked of the creatures in their animal hospital
And drank a toast to the brave little owl, Athena.

THE END

Animal Pouches

Cats and Dogs

the sun likes fun
see how he plays
with golden dogs
on easy breezy days

the moon is fond
of midnight cats
in her spotlight they turn
into acrobats

Adrian Mitchell

Do the Snuffaround

I got a yellow dog
Watch her for hours
She snuffles with her snout
Around the trees and flowers

She snuffs at the grass
She sniffs at the ground
Then she starts digging
Like a natural hound

She does The Snuffaround
She does The Snuffaround
She uses paws and jaws
And claws because
She loves The Snuffaround

Umpteen Pockets

Well she lowers her head
Snuffles at the grime
Then her tail starts wagging
In double time

She holds up one paw
Shoves down her snout
Gonna dig those moles
And rabbits out

She does The Snuffaround
She does The Snuffaround
She uses paws and jaws
Like there ain't no laws
She loves The Snuffaround

Adrian Mitchell

She digs with the left paw
Digs with the right
Digs with both together
She'll be digging all night

She's kicking back earth
Mud clay and sand
She won't stop digging
Till Kangarooland

She does The Snuffaround
She does The Snuffaround
She uses paws and jaws
Doesn't stop for applause
And that's The Snuffaround

Dancing with Dexter

In the long jungly grass on the wild hillside
I met a slim and silvery golden retriever
He was lively and lovely and sixteen months old
And he waved his tail like a magical feather

Well I jumped up and he jumped up
And we bumped our golden chests together
For this is the dance which should always be danced
When one retriever meets another

Up on our hind legs bumping chests
We pushed and pawed and laughed at each other
Till it ended up with a wrestling match
Upside and downside in the heather

by DAISY THE DOG OF PEACE
(Six and three-quarters years old)

Adrian Mitchell

After Performing the Thirteen Secrets of Poetry

After lunch I went to the Library
For my Necessary Nap.

I tried the armchair.
It was too hard.

I tried the twin seats.
They were too awkward.

I tried the four bean bags in the corner
And slept like the Three Bears and Goldilocks.

When I woke up I was given graceful handfuls
Of white and lilac flowers by the Girls in the Class
And felt happy as a Beanbag.

(With love to Crawley Ridge Junior School.)

Surveillance

A Clouded Yellow butterfly
called Joey
was being watched
by a pink-eyed mouse

that mischievous pink-eyed mouse
called Flipper
was being watched
by a stalking black and white kitten

that stalking soft-walking tabby kitten
called Moonlight
was being watched
by a half-asleep Golden Retriever

that half-asleep dreaming Golden Retriever
called Daisy
was being watched
by a white-haired poet

that white-haired puzzling poet
called Adrian
was being watched
by a film camera

the film from that lamppost-mounted camera
called CCTV
was being watched
by a keen police constable

that keen and clever police constable
called Cleopatra Johnson
jumped up and revved up her motorbike
and buzzed round and placed under arrest
Joey Flipper Moonlight Daisy and Adrian
       on suspicion
       of suspiciousness

Big Dog River

      big dog digging
on the heathery mountain
      like a big dogdozer
on the weathery mountain
      big dog digging
      up on Wonky Mountain

tearing up turf
      spraying up stones
      waking up worms
      bouncing up bones

      a blue-eyed marble
      a skull full of earth
      a Roman penny
      but what's that worth?

      deeper and deeper
here's the flinthead of an arrow
and a statue of a goddess
who was shaped like a marrow
      deeper and deeper

Adrian Mitchell

till suddenly *SWASH!*

FLOOF! SCHWOWGOLLY!
and SPLOSHBYGOSH!

out of the belly
of Wonky Mountain
leaps a gynormously
generous fountain

big dog dancing
on the flashing mountain
big dog dancing
on the splashing mountain
big dog laughing
up on Wonky Mountain
and gushing out
rushing out
twenty-four
wonderfall waterfalls
more and more
in a fuddled muddy puddle
up on Wonky Mountain

Umpteen Pockets

and the puddle made a pool
and the pool made a pond
and the pond made a lake
and the lake for heaven's sake
overflowed its bank
and jumped down the flank
of Wonky Mountain

yes the water sprang down
and it leaped along
singing a brand new
river song

Adrian Mitchell

big dog swimming
in the silver river
big dog diving
in the walloping river
swimming underwater
up on Wonky Mountain

and the big dog clambered out
gave a shake and a shiver
and announced to the world: this is Big Dog River!

The Fox

A fox among the shadows of the town,
Should I surrender to the arms of man?
    On the blank icehills lies in wait
    The fighting cold who has thrown down
    His challenge. I'll not imitate
    The feline compromise. I scan
    With warring eyes the servile fate
Of animals who joined the heated town.

Lean-hearted lions in the concrete zoo
Grow bellies, tendons slacken in pale hide,
    Their breath slows to a dying pace.
    Their keepers love them? Tell me who
    Would cage his love in such a place,
    Where only fish are satisfied?
    The keeper has a huntsman's face.
His grasping love would kill me in the zoo.

A scavenger throughout the snowing wind
I peel the sweet bark from the frozen tree
    Or trap the bird with springing jaws.
    The sun retreats out of my mind.

How could I give this waking pause
When death's my sleeping company?
Mad empty, licking at my sores,
I howl this bitter and unloving wind.

Furious in the savage winter day
The crimson riders hounded me from birth
Through landscapes built of thorn and stone.
Though I must be their sudden prey,
Torn to my terror's skeleton,
Or go to the forgotten earth;
I will have hunted too, alone,
I will have wandered in my handsome day.

Four seasons wrestle me, I throw them all
And live to tumble with another year
In love or battle. I'll not fly
From mindless elements and fall
A victim to the keeper's lie.
The field is mine; but still I fear
Strong death, my watching enemy,
Though seasons pass and I survive them all.

The Brave Heifer Stirk

(*Based faithfully on a report from* The Craven Herald and
Pioneer *of July l7th 1970.*)

It is the thirteenth of July
In nineteen-seventy.
Farmers pace Skipton marketplace
Unconscious of their jeopardy.

This heifer stirk in the Auction Mart
Is barely six months old,
But the brain beneath its yellow horns
Intones the words: "I'll not be sold."

The number card is all prepared
On the stirk's back to be stuck,
But the heifer stirk bursts from the ring,
Black mind in spate, bloodstream amok.

Adrian Mitchell

A score of farmers try to pass
Hairy white ropes around its neck
But the stirk upends the best of them
Then splatters down the beck.

It swaggers through King's Foundry Land
To Skipton Hospital
Launches itself and swims across
The Leeds and Liverpool Canal.

Now Betty Thornton's trailer brings
The mother of the stirk to graze.
Monday night is an armistice,
But the dawn sets the stirk ablaze.

Tuesday: and the stirk marches down
To its safe canal again.
It swims about two thousand yards
To disembark at Brewery Lane.

Umpteen Pockets

It slithers down to Eller Beck,
Then stamps downstream until
It stands in the black fifty yards
Of tunnel under Dewhurst's Mill.

For half an hour it drinks the dark,
Then re-emerges, thunderously,
Chased by the staff of the Auction Mart
And Skipton Town Constabulary.

In Gargrave Road it toys with cars
And jellifies the passers-by.
"O save us from this heifer stirk!"
The sad pedestrians cry.

Woodman Terrace becomes its lair…
A trap! This is a cul-de-sac!
Wheedlers advance with jailer's smiles
But the prongs of fury drive them back.

Adrian Mitchell

On the Girls' High School Tennis Courts
Pound those four havoc-wreaking feet.
Men sidle forward, one head is lowered,
Another charge, another mass retreat.

The foreman, Cyril Marshall, comes
From Skipton Auction Mart
With Dave and Tommy Harrison,
Brothers no stirk shall ever part.

To stop a further charge is the attempt
Of Police Sergeant Michael Clemmett,
But, even helped by Constable O'Neil,
There is no way the law can stem it.

Now the stirk's mother is brought again
By trailer to the Tennis Court,
But though the stirk thrice mounts the ramp
It turns back with a rousing snort.

O, Marshall with his lasso all awhirl,
He cannot do the trick.
Nor Clemmett with a wooden form,
Nor O'Neil with a stick.

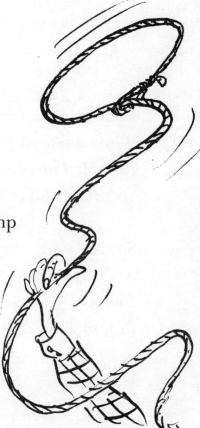

The Force means nothing to a stirk,
Freedom's its only rule.
It shoulders traffic all down Gargrave Road
To reach Ermysted's Grammar School.

Park Avenue, Coach Street, Broughton Road,
It takes at thumping rate,
Then stops beside a bungalow
On the Burnside Estate.

Four hours they've stalked that heifer stirk
While it played fast and loose.
Now Mr Longthorne, of the cattle-truck,
Secures it with a wily noose.

So here's a health to the heifer stirk
And the Skipton steeple-chase,
And may all who love their liberty
Run such a pretty race!

Adrian Mitchell

The New Calf

Beside that dark brown hill of a cow
A chocolate-coloured calf
With a head like a full moon
Lies deep in the Welsh grass.

The new calf lies so still
That you almost think –
But then it shakes its ears
And they don't fall off.
It thinks for a bit
Then shakes its ears again.

Umpteen Pockets

A stately black aunt
Comes round for a visit,
Stepping carefully over
The startled calf.

The back legs of the calf stand up,
Then its front legs, head and all.
It follows its mother to the fence.
They stand and stare at me,
The red baby cord still dangling from the calf.

I greet the new calf quietly:
"Welcome to the field.
Welcome to the world."
The new calf looks at me,

And moos like a mammoth.

Adrian Mitchell

Song of the Red Squirrels

In autumn time
When the nuts are ripe
And the hazel bushes
Are golden and green

We all run down
To the edge of the lake
Where the waters
Are clear and clean

On our little rafts
We paddle away
Past the quacking waterfowl
And we spread out our tails
As bushy red sails
And the autumn breeze
Blows us to the trees
On the Island of the Owl.

Who Won?
(The Hare and Tortoise Race)

It's Springtime! Ring-a-ding-ding time!

Soon be the first of May.
Time to take off your gloomy gloves
And throw your glumboots away.

Bluebells bop around the woods,
Scarecrows sing to their mates,
Streams toboggan down the hills
And the March Hare celebrates.

Have you heard about the mad March Hare?
His legs are like walloping springs.
His ears are tall and elegant
As a furry angel's wings.

He's got a whiskery face
And a wonky sense of humour.
He can travel faster
Than a classroom rumour.

Adrian Mitchell

March Hare swaggers into *The Frog and Toad*
For an acorn-cup of Croaker-Cola.
He puts Leveret Presley on the juke-box –
Yes, he's always been a rock-n-roller.

As the Hare struts around to that funky sound
All the animals give him room
As he shouts: "I'm the fastest creature on earth –
King of Zing and Czar of Zoom!

"You seen greased lightning?
Seen a fighter jet?
I tell you little beasts
You seen nothing yet.

"I'll outrun anybody
That's guaranteed.
I'm silky, streamlined
And built for speed—"

But his speech is rudely interrupted
By a voice from down below,
A drowsy and a growly voice,
Speaking sulkily and slow.

"Who's that chump bumping on my ceiling?
That's no way to behave.
I've been kipping all winter and you woke me up
In my comfortable earthy cave."

Then out of a hollow tree gradually pokes
A grubby, snubby snout.
"One question, brother," the Tortoise grumbles,
"What d'you think you're gabbing about?

"We all know the story of the Tortoise and the Hare –
How the Hare streaks ahead when the race begins;
But good old Slow and Steady keeps plodding along,
The Hare stops and falls asleep – the Tortoise wins.

"Mr Hare, you're what I call the Spasmod Type –
All hop, skip and jump but no Sticktoitivity.
I'm just an old Plodnik, but race against me
And I'll teach you a lesson in Cunning Activity."

All the animals laugh.
The Hare guffaws.
The Tortoise stares.
There's an awful pause.

Then – "Done," says the Hare
And they both crouch low.
The Fox says, "Ready, Steady—"
Off they go!

There's a cloud of dust –
A drumming of paws –
A sound like a zipper –
A scratching of claws.

The spectators try to
Keep their eyes on
The Hare as he hurtles
Over the horizon.

Meanwhile the Tortoise
Is feeling fine,
But he's only just leaving
The starting line.

Raising his right front foot up,
He shifts it forward a few centimetres,
Then lifts his left-hand back foot up
And thus, in bottom gear, he teeters

Like a slo-mo movie shot
Of an expiring whale
Gradually struggling to
The funeral of a snail.

Onward and onward and onward
Dogged as a lazy glacier.
(If you're selecting an Olympic team –
Sludge would be classier.)

So let's cut back to the speeding Hare –
We left him in full flight.
As you might guess – yes, yes –
He's doing more than all right.

Down the mountainside
On his bum he bumps,
Then crosses the river
With kangaroo jumps.

Like a jaguar riding
A motorbike.
Like a rocketship racing
A lightning strike.

Adrian Mitchell

Dashing and flashing
And whizzing and fizzing.
Plunging and lunging
And ripping and zipping.

Hurrying, scurrying,
Pounding, bounding,
Springing, zinging,
Heltering, skeltering.

A mile below him –
There's the winning post –
No stopping him now –
He's there – almost –

But, before his last sprint,
The Hare thinks it best
To relax and give his
Famous legs a rest.

So he stretches and rolls
In the grass by a stream
And he yawns and is lost
In a beautiful dream

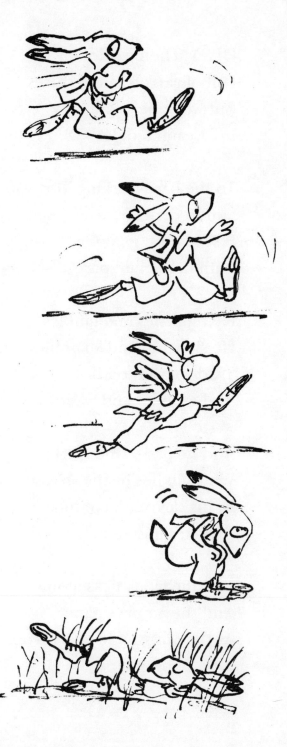

Of a kitchen garden
Full of carrots and lettuces –
But while he's so happy
In Dreamland, let's whizz

To the hard-working Tortoise
Still in the race,
P l o d d i n g along
With deliberate pace.

He mooches and ambles.
He slouches and shambles,
Trudges and toddles,
And wobbles and waddles.

And he passes the Hare
Who still lies by the stream
In his carrot and lettuce
Devouring dream,

And the clock ticks along
And the animals gape
As the Tortoise breaks through
The winning tape.

He staggers, exhausted,
And for his success
Receives the Gold Medal
From the Hedgehog Princess.

She praises the Tortoise
In tones warm and gushing.
Then they hear the Hare laugh
Like a toilet flushing.

Says the Tortoise: "Laugh on,
Laugh on till you burst.
But I won the race –
I came in first!"

Says the Hare: "I saw you
On the road.
You looked like your shell
Was about to explode.

"You had dust in your lungs
And corns on your feet –
Do you call that
A winning athlete?

"But did you see me
Running at all?
I was leaping faster
Than a waterfall.

"I galloped and tap-danced
And sang to the crowd.
I turned back-somersaults
And surfed on a cloud.

"So don't try and tell me
That you won –
You didn't even
Enjoy the run!

"If you want to find out
Which of us won
Ask yourself this question:
Who had the most fun?"

Adrian Mitchell

The Lost Animal Home

On a slope beside the growling sea
with blue doors and a greeny dome
and caves for shelter and a helter-skelter
stands the Lost Animal Home.

Oh who's that knocking at the shiny blue door
with a fist that goes bomp bomp bomp?
Let me in from the frost, for I'm lost as lost
And miles from my dear old swamp.

No room! No room! You're a Crocodile
and that's not an animal,
any more than a copper or a gobstopper
or a red-hot cannonball.

Umpteen Pockets

Why not slither away towards Egypt
down Floppermost Hill and jog
till you come face to face with the squashumptious place
which is know as All Fours Bog.

That's not my swamp, cried the Lost Crocodile
and his tears fell like glassy pears.
Let me into the Lost Animal Home
where I may forget all my cares.

The Lost Stork examined the Crocodile's teeth –
They're remarkably strong and clean.
Two hundred and three, all sharp as can be,
not a filling to be seen!

The Lost Frog looked over the Crocodile's skin
from his nostrils back to his tail –
He is wonderfully green and warty
and muscular and male.

Should the softhearted Animals let him come in?
They decided to take a vote
And all of them said – Let's give him a bed –
all except for the Little Lost Goat,

Oh, how they celebrated that night!
The band was called Serious Sheep.
They hopped and they pranced till they fell where they danced
in an Animal heap of sleep.

But when the Lost Cockerel woke them at dawn
they were all mystified to note
that their friend the Lost Crocodile was gone –
and so was the Little Lost Goat.

Adrian Mitchell

The English Game

Of all the great games ever practised or known
Cricket stands tall in a class of its own
And wherever the leather by willow is smitten
The Cricketing nation all fear is Great Britain!

    (chorus)
      So bash me a boundary, snatch me a catch,
      I wager we'll triumph in every match.
      So bowl me a bouncer and whack down that wicket
      And show the whole world how old England plays Cricket.

Those Springboks and Kiwis are all doomed to failure
And so are the big-talking boys from Australia,
Sri Lanka surrenders, the Windies get windier
As Pakistan topples and under goes India.

    (chorus)
      So bash me a boundary, snatch me a catch – etc.

        by Adrian Mitchell (half-English)

The Scottish Sport

The bonniest sport in the world I must sing
All sportsmen acknowledge that fitba's the King
And wherever a boot taks a swing at the ball
It's Scotland the Brave that's the flower of them all.

(chorus)
    The beautiful game was by Scotland invented
    The game that has driven the world half demented
    Forget aboot Germany, also Brazil –
    When Scotland plays England it's always six-nil!

Ye can talk of your Cruyffs, Bobby Robsons and Peles –
Compared with oor Scots, there's nae fire in their bellies.
The soccer world trembles when our team unleash
The Sons of Bill Shankley and Kenny Dalglish!

(chorus)
    The beautiful game was by Scotland invented – etc.

by Adrian Mitchell (half-Scottish)

Adrian Mitchell

Full English Breakfast

Full English Breakfast
Sent from above
Butter and toast and beans
Chunky old marmalade
That's what we love
That is what England means
Full English Breakfast
Doing its best
Marching as if to war
Full English Breakfast
Standing the test
Two eggs and bacon
If I'm not mistaken
That is what England's for

Umpteen Pockets

Black pudding
Plum jam
Pass the cornflakes to Pam
Grilled mushrooms
Fried bread
How's your gumboil Uncle Fred?
A nice pair
Of kippers
That smell like old slippers
Have a sausage
Eat your fill
Till you see a Vision of the Holy Grill…

Full English Breakfast
Flowing and free
Pride of the Seven Seas
Full English Breakfast
Strong English tea
Sadie likes three lumps please
Full English Breakfast
Doing its bit
Filling the English tum
England was made for Man
As God's own Frying Pan
It's the Full Monty, Mum!

Patriotic Song

What colour are a Llama's pyjamas
    When that old Moon is new?
      What colour are the pants
        Of the Elephants
And the hue of the shoe of a Gnu?

Does a Bean wear green or aquamarine?
    Tell me, tell me true.
  Now, I don't want to be a bore
  But if they're British to the core
Well, they're Red, White and Blue all through!

The Postman's Palace

Deep down in France is the village of Hauterives,
A village as quiet
As a heap of stones by the roadside…
To the brave heart, nothing is impossible.

A new postman came to Hauterives
And he was known as Le Facteur Cheval
Which means, in English, Postman Horse.
Time does not pass, but we do.

Adrian Mitchell

One night Postman Horse dreamed himself a dream
And in it he saw, at the bottom of his garden,
A wonderful palace of stairways and towers
Decorated with trees and fruit made of stone
And camels and giants and goddesses and elephants.
Out of art, out of a dream, out of energy.

Next day Postman Horse was on his rounds
When he tripped over an odd-shaped stone.
He took it home in his wooden wheelbarrow,
Set it on the ground in his garden, and smiled.
This is where the dream becomes reality.

Postman Horse began to build.
Every day on his rounds he found amazing stones.
Every day after work he collected them.
Carefully, each evening, he cemented the stones together.
Gradually the palace of his dreams began to rise.
To the brave heart, nothing is impossible.

Umpteen Pockets

After ten thousand days of work
In the freezer of winter, the oven of summer,
After thirty-three back-breaking years of work
The palace was finished, with its stairways and towers
Decorated with trees and fruit made of stone
And camels and giants and goddesses and elephants.
Postman Horse wrote on panels of cement:

All that you see as you pass by
Is the work of a peasant,
The work of one man alone.
Time does not pass, but we do.

I have seen the palaces
Of the Kings of England, France and Russia.
They were magnificent and dead.
But deep down in France is the village of Hauterives
And from its earth there rises
A wonderful palace built out of dreams
Where Postman Horse inscribed these words:

To the brave heart, nothing is impossible.
Time does not pass, but we do.
Out of art, out of a dream, out of energy.
This is where the dream becomes reality.

Adrian Mitchell

Runny Honey

Grab some pollen Mister Bumblebee
Build a honeycomb and drop it on me
I want that
Runny Honey
Runny Honey
Makes my tummy feel fine and funny

Bumblebee Bumblebee don't be late
I'm not the kind of Bear likes to wait
Bring me that
Runny Honey
Runny Honey
Makes my tummy feel fine and funny

Umpteen Pockets

Back in the cave my Mama used to say
You need that honey seven times a day
I asked her if she meant the solid kind
She said: Bear – are you out of your mind?

You need

Runny Honey
Runny Honey
Go slurp slurp slurp

Then give a sweet burp

And eat that honey

While it's runny Sonny
That'll make your tummy feel fine fine fine

And funny!

Adrian Mitchell

Purple Valley

Down in Purple Valley
Under a fingernail moon
The woollycoated children
Skate on Sugary Lagoon.

I went and told their Mother
She hit me with an inkpot.
I went and told their Father
He said I was a stinkpot.

I went and told the Trumpeter
He played a bugle call
So I went and sailed my swan-shaped boat
Over the waterfall.

Hampstead Heath

Dawn. A pink pond. A rabbit sniffs the dew
And the trees stretch their brawny arms
And meadows raise their faces to the sky,
Adam smiles up at Eve. And all is new.

The Song of the Faithful Old Fridge

When She opens my door.
My light comes on.
But it goeth out
When She is gone.

Adrian Mitchell

All Over the Violet Snow

(*from* The Snow Queen)

Every year at this time
The waters of the lake
Are changed in a wonderful way,
And the skates come out
From under the stairs
And the town comes out to play.

Skidding and sliding,
Collapsing, colliding
And leaping and gliding
    We go.
Dodging and veering
And wildly careering
All over the violet snow.

Wheeling and whirling
And crashing and curling
And turning and twirling
    We go.
We're bawling and calling
And fooling and falling
All over the violet snow.

Down below
Fishes are sleeping
A fishy kind of sleep.
Down below
Beetles are creeping
An underwater creep.
Down below
Slimy weeds clinging,
Mermaids are singing,
There's slushy old
Squashy old mud –

But up here –
    Swaying and slipping
    And grabbing and gripping
    And tramping and tripping
       We go.
Joking and jumping,
Deliberately bumping,
All over the violet,
Over the violet,
Over the violet snow…

Adrian Mitchell

To All Our Friends

August
blue seas for ever
a spicy breeze
bears us towards an ancient island

the harbour opens its arms to us
in an embrace
of boats with clinking masts
brown children leaping over ropes
donkeys fishermen dogs
women with baby bundles
shadow cats
and the sun
shining down upon a maze
of whitewashed alleys
leading up towards
bright domes and shining towers
and beyond all these
the dark hills of enchantment

Umpteen Pockets

we have come home
to the island which we've been creating
for so many years
with our buckets and spades

and here we all stand
with salt spray in our eyes
makers of dreamcakes and mudpies

Adrian Mitchell

Peace and Pancakes

(*from* The Fear Brigade)

The Old World began with a Big Bang
     A Big Bang, A Big Bang.
The New World begins with a Big Song
     A Big Song, A Big Song.

It's got a strong beat, like your heartbeat,
So stomp out that beat – use your own two feet
For a Big Song of Pancakes and Peace
A Big Song – everybody sing along!

Everybody loves Pancakes
And everybody loves Peace.
You can find Pancakes all round the world
North South West and East.

    Dosas for breakfast in India
    With spicy veg in the middle.
    Canadian maple syrup
    On buckwheat cakes hot off the griddle.
       Long live Peace and Pancakes!

The Greeks make pancakes with semolina.
Russians make their blinis with yeast.
Red-hot quesadillas in Mexico City –
Yes Pancakes turn any meal into a feast!
    Long live Peace and Pancakes!

In Beijing they fill pancakes
With plum sauce and roast duck.
Every Shrove Tuesday in England
My pancake always gets stuck! Bad luck!
    Long live Peace and Pancakes!

Koreans call their pancakes pa'chon
And cook 'em with sesame seeds.
The Romans serve cannelloni.
Pancakes are the banquet everyone needs.
    Long live Peace and Pancakes!

South Africa's banana chapattis,
Brittany's crepes Suzettes.
Every woman and man from Chile to Japan,
They're eating all they can get.

Adrian Mitchell

Everybody loves Pancakes
    And everybody loves Peace.
You can find Pancakes all round the world
North South West and East.

Long live the planet Earth
Long live the Animals
Long live the Birds and Fishes
Long live the Forests and the Oceans

Long live the Man
Long live the Woman
Who use both Courage and Compassion
Long live their Children

    Long live Peace!
    Long live Peace!
    Long live Peace and Pancakes!

UMPTEEN POCKETS

Index of First Lines

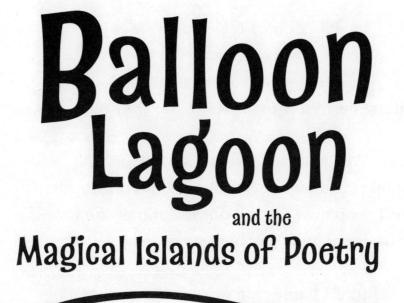

Balloon Lagoon
and the
Magical Islands of Poetry

Magic Islands

Whenever I feel super-brave
I ghost away from my PC
To follow the secret, sandy path
Leading down to the shores of the Daydream Sea.

And I sail away in my Skylark boat
While our blue-green sail is followed by birds
And I drop my wide net down through the waves
In the hope of catching some fishy words.

But if I haul some word-fishes aboard
I pick the best ones out of the heap
And draw their portraits lovingly –
Then throw them all back into the deep.

Sail on, sail on, my little boat,
Round this shining archipelago.
Look down – the underwater city
Of great Atlantis, far below.

Sail on, sail on, the mermaids sing,
A lighthouse sword cuts through the dark.
The fountain of the Great White Whale!
The Woofmiaou Isles where purr meets bark!

We'll ride the whirlpools and the storms,
We'll dodge Iceberg Academy too
And fight the Giant Octopus
And Captain Bloodshot's desperate Crew.

Balloon Lagoon, Elephantasia,
Spookalulu where the zombies crawl.
Mysteriosa and The Rampages –
My boat and I visit them all.

The Skylark's eager to be off,
So hop on board and sail with me
Together we'll explore today
The Magic Islands of Poetry.

BALLOON LAGOON

CONTENTS

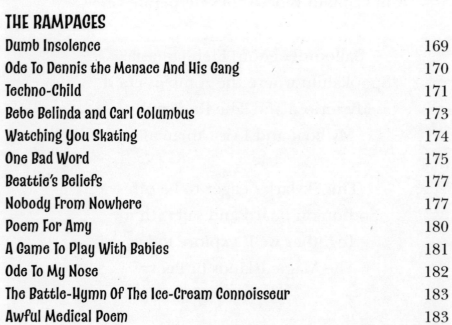

ELEPHANTASIA

SPOOKALULU

BALLOON LAGOON

Mysteriosa

secret land of magic,
mind-mazes and marmalade

The Woman of Water

There once was a woman of water
Refused a Wizard her hand.

So he took the tears of a statue
And the weight from a grain of sand
And he squeezed the sap from a comet
And the height from a cypress tree
And he drained the dark from midnight
And he charmed the brains from a bee
And he soured the mixture with thunder
And stirred it with ice from hell
And the woman of water drank it down
And she changed into a well.

There once was a woman of water
Who was changed into a well
And the well smiled up at the Wizard
And down down down that old Wizard fell...

Adrian Mitchell

Stufferation

Lovers lie around in it
Broken glass is found in it
Grass
I like that stuff

Tuna fish get trapped in it
Legs come wrapped in it
Nylon
I like that stuff

Eskimos and tramps chew it
Madame Tussaud gave status to it
Wax
I like that stuff

Elephants get sprayed with it
Scotch is made with it
Water
I like that stuff

Umpteen Pockets

Clergy are dumbfounded by it
Bones are surrounded by it
Flesh
I like that stuff

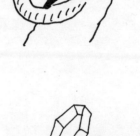

Harps are strung with it
Mattresses are sprung with it
Wire
I like that stuff

Carpenters make cots of it
Undertakers use lots of it
Wood
I like that stuff

Dirty cigarettes are lit by it
Pensioners get happy when they sit by it
Fire
I like that stuff

Johnny Dankworth's alto is made of it, most of it*
Scoobdidoo is composed of it**
Plastic
I like that stuff

Adrian Mitchell

Elvis kept it in his left-hand pocket
Little Richard made it zoom like a rocket
Rock 'n' Roll
Ooh my soul
I like that stuff

Apemen take it to make them hairier
I ate a ton of it in Bulgaria
Yoghurt
I like that stuff

Man-made fibres and raw materials
Old rolled gold and breakfast cereals
Platinum linoleum
I like that stuff

Umpteen Pockets

Skin on my hands
Hair on my head
Toenails on my feet
And linen on the bed

Well I like that stuff
Yes I like that stuff
The earth
Is made of earth
And I like that stuff

*Jazz musician John Dankworth used to play a plastic saxophone.

**Scoobdidoo was a fistful of kind of multi-coloured pieces of plastic which were a playground craze in the 1950s. It was a sad sort of toy, nothing like the exciting Hula Hoop of the same period.

Adrian Mitchell

Mesopotamia

I dreamed I was sailing on dusty waters
Mesopotamia Mesopotamia
There were two yellow rivers merged into one river
Mesopotamia Mesopotamia
My boat had a woven cabin for shade
And a golden double sail like an eagle in flight
And a woman who sang to me like marmalade
As we sailed in the direction of the night

Nothingmas Day

No it wasn't.
It was Nothingmas Eve and all the children in Notown were not
tingling with excitement as they lay unawake in their heaps.
D
  o
    w
      n
        s
          t
            a
              i
                r

           s their parents were busily not placing
the last crackermugs, glimmerslips and sweetlumps on the
Nothingmas Tree.

Hey! But what was that invisible trail of chummy sparks
or vaulting stars across the sky?
      Father Nothingmas – drawn by 18 or 21 rainmaidens!
      Father Nothingmas – his sackbut bulging with air!
      Father Nothingmas – was not on his way!
(From the streets of the snowless town came the quiet of
unsung carols and the merry silence of the steeple bell.)

Adrian Mitchell

Next morning the children did not fountain out of bed with cries of WHOOPERATION! They picked up their Nothingmas Stockings and with traditional quiperamas such as: "Look what I haven't got! It's just what I didn't want!" pulled their stockings on their ordinary legs.

For breakfast they ate – breakfast.

After woods they all avoided the Nothingmas Tree, where Daddy, his face failing to beam like a leaky torch, was not distributing gemgames, sodaguns, golly-trolleys, jars of humdrums and packets of slubberated croakers.

Off, off, off went the children to school, soaking each other with no howls of "Merry Nothingmas and a Happy No Year!", and not pulping each other with no-balls.

At school Miss Whatnot taught them how to write
No Thank You Letters.

Home they burrowed for Nothingmas Dinner.
The table was not groaning under all manner of
    NO TURKEY
    NO SPICED HAM
    NO SPROUTS
    NO CRANBERRY JELLYSAUCE
    NO NOT NOWT
There was not one (1) shoot of glee as the Nothingmas
Pudding, unlit, was not brought in. Mince pies were not
available, nor was there any demand for them.

Then, as another Nothingmas clobbered to a close, they all
haggled off to bed where they slept happily never after.

    and that is not the end of the story...

Adrian Mitchell

My Last Nature Walk

I strode among the clumihacken
Where scrubble nudges to the barfter
Till I whumped into, hidden in the bracken,
A groolted after-laughter-rafter.
(For milty Wah-Zohs do guffaw
Upon a laughter-rafter perch.
But after laughter they balore
Unto a second beam to gurch.)
Yet here was but one gollamonce!
I glumped upon the after-laughter-rafter.
Where was its other-brother? Oh! My bonce!
The Wah-Zohs blammed it with a laughter-rafter.

Moral: Never gamble on a bramble ramble.

Glossary:
clumihacken – the old stalks of wild Brussels sprouts
scrubble – unusually tall moss, often scuffed
the barfter – the height at which low clouds cruise
to whump – to bump into, winding oneself in the process
groolted – cunningly engraved with the portraits of little-known
*   and famous barbers*
milty – clean but mean-minded
Wah-Zohs – French birds, sometimes spelt Oiseaux
to balore – to hover fatly downwards
to gurch – to recover from cheerfulness
gollamonce – a thing that is sought for desperately, although
*   there is no good reason for finding it*
to glump – to glump
to blam – to shonk on the cloddle

The Village Pond Has Good Words For Everybody

to the grass it says   green

to the swan it says   whitest

to the breeze   ripples

to the heron   welcome

to the summer   coolness

to the winter   ice

to the fishes   green whitest

ripples welcome

coolness ice home

Adrian Mitchell

Construction Kit Paint Invention

Dip the brush provided in your can
Of Detacho-Paint.
Detacho-Paint the surface
Of the limb or digit or organ required.
Allow half an hour
For the subtle molecular change
Brought about by Detacho-Paint.
Now you can painlessly remove, by hand,
That limb, digit or organ.

You can take off your fingers one by one
And plant them in your armpits.
You can take off your nose
And stick it to the back of your neck.
You can take off your arms and legs
And swap them with your friends.
They still work fine.
They've still got feelings.
Switch your ears for your feet with Detacho-Paint.
Take off your head and have a good game
Of volley-ball with your bonce.

155

Umpteen Pockets

I remember Meccano
With its flat little spanners
And fiddly nuts and bolts
And scraping the paint of red and blue girders
And the sadness of Meccano animals,
So skeletal, so full of holes,
So unlike anything except Meccano.

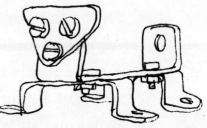

And I remember my Bayko Building Set,
With its silver rods rising hopefully
From a green bakelite base,
Waiting for red bricks, white bricks and green bricks
To be slid down into place between them
Eventually forming a rather forbidding model
Of a suburban public convenience.

I even remember Minibrix,
Those ceramic bricks the size of fingernails,
The colour of baked beans,
Which had to be stuck into place with toy cement
And soaked apart again, but that took months...

Adrian Mitchell

I even remember a primitive kind of Lego
Made of smelly red rubber
And also other, sillier construction kits
Involving warped wooden rods, elastic bands
And clockwork motors.
All of them came in boxes
Picturing boys in shorts with polished hair
Dwarfed by models of steam engines and Eiffel Towers.
All of them defeated me utterly, utterly.

But now I have my happy Revenge
For I can become a construction kit myself.
I simply dip the brush into Detacho-Paint
And paint the surface
Of my body, my limbs, my head
And proceed, gradually, with great pleasure
To take myself to pieces.

And then I put myself together again
To form an entirely different model.

Watch Your Step – I'm Drenched

In Manchester there are a thousand puddles.
Bus-queue puddles poised on slanting paving stones,
Railway puddles slouching outside stations,
Cinema puddles in ambush at the exits,
Zebra-crossing puddles in dips of the dark stripes –
They lurk in the murk
Of the north-western evening
For the sake of their notorious joke,
Their only joke – to soak
The tights or trousers of the citizens.
Each splash and consequent curse is echoed by
One thousand dark Mancunian puddle chuckles.
In Manchester there lives the King of Puddles,
Master of Miniature Muck Lakes,
The Shah of Slosh, Splendifero of Splash,
Prince, Pasha and Pope of Puddledom.
Where? Somewhere. The rain-headed ruler
Lies doggo, incognito,
Disguised as an average, accidental mini-pool.

He is as scared as any other emperor,
For one night, all his soiled and soggy victims
Might storm his streets, assassination in their minds,
A thousand rolls of blotting paper in their hands,
And drink his shadowed, one-joke life away.

Maya's Song

Face after face after face after face –
The city is a most faceful place.
So I run to the countryside scenery
And chameleon into its greenery.
O the faces of cities both jagged and kind
Go gently slipping out of my mind
And the only face I can see pretty soon
Is the so-what face of the snowy moon.

Patchwork Rap

I'm a touch lazy
Don't like doing much work
But often get the itch
To pitch into some patchwork
It may be a hotchpotch
Like fretwork or such work
When I slouch on my couch
And I fetch out my patchwork

First I snatch a patch
From the batch in my pouch
But the patch doesn't match
The patches on my patchwork
So I catch another patch
From the batch in my satchel
And this one matches
The patches on my patchwork

So I take my patch
Attach it with stitches
Patch against patch
Where the patchwork matches
But if it doesn't match
Even after it's attached
Then the mismatched stitch
Has to be detached...

You know
I don't like thatchwork
Don't like ditchwork
Only kind I favour
Is my patchwork stitchwork
And soon my patchwork's
Going like clockwork
Sharper than a pitchfork
Neater than brickwork
Hotter than a firework
Cooler than a waxwork

Umpteen Pockets

So I snatch a patch
From the batch in my pouch
But the patch doesn't match
The patches on my patchwork
So I catch another patch
From the batch in my satchel
And this one matches
The patches on my patchwork
So I take my patch
Attach it with stitches
Patch against patch
Where the patchwork matches
And I keep on patching
Till everything's matching
And I keep on stitching
Till I've filled up the kitchen
With my rich rich rich rich
Wider than a soccer pitch
Wonderful colourful magical patchwork quilt!

Now which stitch is which?

Adrian Mitchell

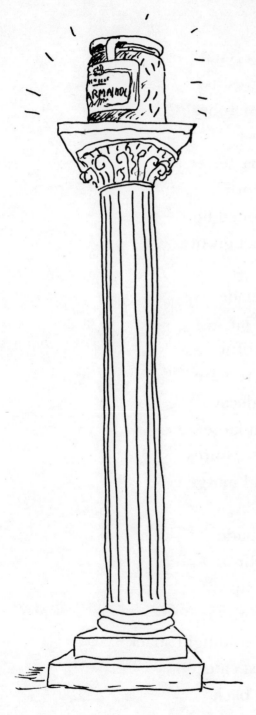

A Sticky End

Jar of marmalade
Marmalade jar
What a beautiful
Shining person you are
For the marmalade germs
Are mortified
To see those dark
Orangey chunks inside
Which recline in the depths
Of a succulent glade
In a miniature jungle
Of marmalade

Umpteen Pockets

Like a castle of crystal
Your glass wall resists
The beating of microbes'
Puny fists
And a million bacteria
Cannot remove
Your golden-rimmed lid
From its stickysweet groove

Jar of marmalade
Marmalade jar
What a beautiful
Shining person you are
You defy the decay
Of the world at large
To save all your treasures
For my bread and marge

Jar of marmalade
Jar of might
I lifted you up
The other night
For I fancied a just-after-midnight snack
But alas! the last eater
Who put you back

Adrian Mitchell

Had only replaced
And not screwed down the lid
By which I raised you
And so in mid-
Air you sadly
Detached yourself
And bounced askance
From a lower-down shelf
And crashed to a splintery, splungey doom
On the cruel tiles
Of the gobsmacked room

Jar as bright
As the Land of Oz
What a beautiful
Shining person you was

Yes

A smile says: Yes.
A heart says: Blood.
When the rain says: Drink,
The earth says: Mud.

The kangaroo says: Trampoline.
Giraffes say: Tree.
A bus says: Us,
While a car says: Me.

Lemon trees say: Lemons.
A jug says: Lemonade.
The villain says: You're wonderful.
The hero: I'm afraid.

The forest says: Hide and Seek.
The grass says: Green and Grow.
The railway says: Maybe.
The prison says: No.

Adrian Mitchell

The millionaire says: Take.
The beggar says: Give.
The soldier cries: Mother!
The baby sings: Live.

The river says: Come with me.
The moon says: Bless.
The stars say: Enjoy the light.
The sun says: Yes.

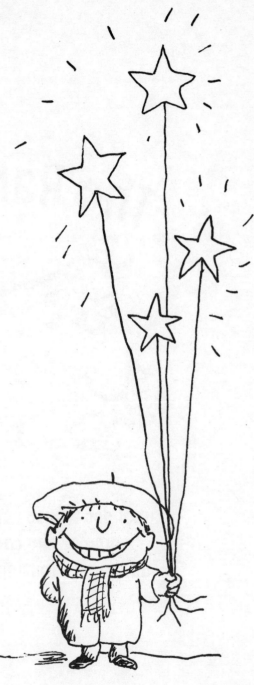

The Rampages

amongst whose ragged rocks run riot
some of the toughest, daftest
and most amazing kids still at large

Adrian Mitchell

Dumb Insolence

I'm big for ten years old
Maybe that's why they get at me

Teachers, parents, cops
Always getting at me

When they get at me

I don't hit 'em
They can do you for that

I don't swear at 'em
They can do you for that

I stick my hands in my pockets
And stare at them

And while I stare at them
I think about sick

They call it dumb insolence
They don't like it
But they can't do you for it

Ode To Dennis The Menace And His Gang

There are Four Seasons of the Beano:
    Chocolate Eggs!
        Sandcastle Contest!
            Fireworks!
                and
                    Xmas Stocking!
Oh Xmas Stocking! Favourite Season!
When all along the top of the fat word

            BEANO

    lies
like a generous layer of icing on the cakes in a box of tuck
            Snow! As in Snowmen!
            Snow! As in Snowballs!

                Snow!
Snow!   Snow!   Snow!
        which falls and drifts in every Reader's dreams

Adrian Mitchell

Techno-Child

My dad was a kung fu fighter in a video game called
      Death Cult Army
He lurked around on the seventh level waiting for smug
      contestants so he could chop them up like salami
He was good for nothing but kick jab punch gouge headbutt
      kick in the bum
And all his friends were stuperollificated when he fell in love
      and married my mum

My mum was a thirty-two colour hologram at a Medical
      Convention in Beverly Hills
She represented the Statue of Liberty and she advertised
      Anti-Indigestion Pills
She was half the size of the statue itself and the tourists
      she attracted were fewer
And if you ever reached out to touch her robes, well
      your hand just went straight through her

They met in the Robocop Theme Park on a hullabaloo
      of a night
When my dad saw off some Gremlins on Camels who
      had challenged mum to a fight

Umpteen Pockets

They sat together and watched the moon from a
      swing-chair on Popeye's porch
Then my father proposed in Japanese and my mother
      she dropped her torch

They were married and put on a floppy disc by
      the Bishop of IBM
Pac-Man, Count Duckula and all the Power Rangers
      came and celebrated with them
The fun was going ballistic but it nearly ended
      in tears
For those old Space Invaders started a ruck with
      the Mortal Kombateers

Since my mum's a mirage of electrons and my dad
      is strictly 2-D
You may wonder how I was born at all in this
      Virtual Reality
Well they're close as a Mouse and its Mouse-mat
      and they taught me just what I should do –
I fight video-gamesters and indigestion with
      pills and a torch and kung fu.

Adrian Mitchell

Bebe Belinda And Carl Columbus
(Verses for Laura)

There was a girl who threw bananas about
When she couldn't get bananas she threw baseball bats about
When she couldn't get baseball bats she threw big blue
      beehives about
And her name was Bebe, Bebe Belinda

There was a boy who threw cuckoo clocks about
When he couldn't find cuckoo clocks he threw cucumbers about
When he couldn't find cucumbers he went crackers and threw
      christening cakes about
And his name was Carl, Carl Columbus

In Hanover Terrace, that magical place,
Bebe and Carl met, face to red face.
She bust his cuckoo clock with a bunch of bananas.
In a swashbuckling sword fight his cucumber cutlass
Carved her baseball bat to bits.
She bashed him on the bonce with her best blue beehive
But he craftily crowned her with a christening cake.

And they left it to me, old Lizzie Lush
To clean up the street with my scrubbing brush.

Watching You Skating

I see two skates
Blue sliding into silver
Silver gliding into blue

I see two moons
One moon reflected in each of the skates
Carrying you

You zip across the blue and silver pond
I am wonderfully fond
Of the moon and the moon-faced pond and you

174

Adrian Mitchell

One Bad Word

(To my Black friends and their children and others
who are sometimes taunted with ugly names by fools.)

You call me that bad word
That one bad word
That bad word weighs a thousand tonne
That one bad word burns my skin all over
You call me one bad word
That word makes my mother
Cast down her eyes in shame
Makes my father
Deny his own name
Makes my brother
Turn and fight like a demon
Makes my sister
Spend her life in bad dreaming

So call me one bad word
And you don't know what will happen
It could be tears it could be blood
It could be storm
It could be silence
It could be a rage
Hot enough to burn the whole town down

Could be a stampede of elephants
Through your back garden
And into your mother's
Frilly perfume sitting room
Could be zombie nightmares
Every night for the rest
Of your natural life
Could be all your food
From this day on
Will taste of rotten fishheads
Could be anything
Could be the end of the world
But mostly likely
This will follow:

I'll stare at you
For one cold second
And then I'll turn and walk away from you
Leaving you alone with yourself
And your one bad word

Adrian Mitchell

Beattie's Beliefs

God made the world
God made ballet
God made everything

except fireworks

Nobody From Nowhere

The Nurse she said:
What you doing in bed?
I said: nothing.
The Matron came
And asked: What's your name?
I said: nobody.
The Student with his comb
Said: Where's your home?
I said: nowhere.
The Doctor prodded,
The Doctor nodded.
I heard the Doctor say:
Who are you anyway?
I said: nobody.

177

Umpteen Pockets

You see, I was feeling so miserable
I was trying to turn inviserable.
Then they gave me a pill and a big mug of tea
And I floated away on a blackcurrant sea
Up a cliff of cream buns
To a sky full of suns

And I don't know how it happened
But I know I was rapping
Yes flying over London
With my pyjamas flapping

I was munching marshmallows
In the marshes of Mars
And I whooshed through the Milky Way's
Sherbet of stars
Then I was hopping on the Moon
With my galactic Mum
Till I tripped on some Krypton
And landed on my bum.

Adrian Mitchell

And my eyes began to open
And I heard the Nurse say:
You've had your operation –
How are you today?
Nobody from Nowhere,
    Do you feel OK?

I'm not Nobody
From Nowhere, mate,
I'm the Famous Somebody
And I feel great
And I just had a brilliant
    Operation Dream
And so, by golly,
Wheel me in a trolley
Full of Planetary Pizza
Space Jelly and Moony Ice Cream.

Westminster Children's Hospital

Poem For Amy

Poetry can be a lonely walk
Down a dark forest pathway
Without an end.
So it lifts the heart to see the brightness
Of a welcoming new friend.

What's that wonderful, warmful light
Shining out a thousand miles?
All the animals of the world start dancing –
When Amy smiles.

Adrian Mitchell

A Game To Play With Babies

Ring the bell – ding ding
Press the buzzer – bzzzzzz
Knock at the door – knock knock
And walk in – oh, no thank you!

(The way to play. Ring the bell – pull the earlobe.
Press the buzzer – press the tip of the nose.
Knock at the door – tap the forehead.
And walk in – put your little finger in mouth and withdraw
        it quickly before you're bitten saying, "Oh, no thank you!"
It's best to demonstrate all these movements and words
on yourself a few times until the baby has got the idea.
Then you try the baby's earlobe, nose, forehead and mouth,
but very gently. Be careful with the fourth move – some
babies have tiger teeth. You will find that most babies
enjoy this game, especially after the twentieth repetition.)

Ode To My Nose

O Nose
Why perch upon my Face?
Could you not find
A better place?

You jut between
One Eye and tother
So neither Eye
Can see his Brother.

An easy target
For the hostile Fist.
You're an obstruction
When I want to be kissed.

And when you run
It's always South
Over my top lip
Into my Mouth.

O Nose
Why perch upon my Face?

Could you discover
No better place?

My Nose replied:
Up here I have come
As far as possible
From your Bum.

The Battle-Hymn Of The Ice-Cream Connoisseur

Mine eyes have seen the glory of Pink Fudge Sundaes
I guzzle 'em on Saturdays and slurp on Mondays
I smuggle 'em to chapel in my Grandma's undies
As my stomach rumbles on.

Awful Medical Poem

If I had a rusty concrete mixer
I would fill it with Murcheson's Cough Elixir.
Doesn't the thought of it make you sick, sir?

Fruit Jokes

The satsuma
Has no sense of humour
But a fig'll
Giggle

My Yellow Jumper

When I ride a banana
At the local gymkhana
I usually win
By a skin

Adrian Mitchell

Deep Sherbet

deep sherbet
in a cardboard
cylinder
printed red
and yellow

used to poke
my liquorice
tube down through
the top and sucked

and when the sherbet
hit the spittle
on my palate –
that's when the fizz began

The Woofmiaou Isles

home of noble-minded dogs
and conniving cats

Adrian Mitchell

In The Country With Billie

With both hands I lift her
High over my hat
And she growls as I call her
My Flying Cat,

Then down to my shoulder
And round my back
She curls like a scarf
Of white and black.

As I climb through the woods
In my purring scarf
Why do the squirrels
And hedgehogs laugh?

She keeps me warm
When the rain blows chilly –
My black-coated, white-booted
Friend called Billie.

Singapore Sausage Cat

Behold the cat
the cat full of sausage
his ears do slope backwards
his coat's full of glossage

His whiskers extend
like happy antennae
he would count his blessings
but they are too many

He unfoldeth his limbs
he displayeth his fur
he narrows his eyes
and begins to purr

And his purring is smooth
as an old tree's mossage –
Behold the cat
who is full of sausage

Adrian Mitchell

I Walk Two Dogs

(for Ella and Judy)

I walk two dogs.
On her black lead and chain
Trots my Marilyn Monroe retriever
With all her golden feathers flowing.

I walk two dogs.
On her small red lead
Runs an old Jack Russell like a country aunt.
Just above her tail she wears a large black blot
Which indicates where she likes to be patted.

I walk two dogs,
Their paths are intertwined.
When we reach Hampstead Heath and their freedom
They glance around, making up their minds
Where we're supposed to go.

Monroe's an archaeologist,
Her aunt is an explorer,
So the retriever digs
While the Jack Russell gets as lost as she can.
I go for walks in two directions at once,
Though sometimes they graze on the scents in the grass,
Muzzles together in the smoky early morning.

I call them to me, I fix their leads.
As I follow them home I feel like the sail
Of a ship of gold and black and white.
I walk two dogs
I walk two dogs
I walk them on two leads
Held in one hand

Footnote To "I Walk Two Dogs"

I boastfully wrote "I Walk Two Dogs"
Then went to catch a bus and passed a fellow
Walking six greyhounds on their leads
Dressed in long coats of black and yellow.
They were strong and perfectly-formed and clean
Like the components of a submarine.

Adrian Mitchell

For Golden Ella

At four in the morning
With furry tread
My good dog climbs
Aboard my bed

She lays her chin
In my open palm
Now neither of us
Can come to harm

In my open hand
Her long jaw seems
Like a shifting weight
As she chews at her dreams
From the coolness
Of her nose
The blessing of
Her breathing glows

And the bad night
Vampires disappear
As my wrist is tickled
By her ear

To My Dog

This gentle beast
This golden beast
laid her long chin
along my wrist

and my wrist
is branded
with her love
and trust

and the salt of my cheek
is hers to lick
so long as I
or she shall last

A Poem For Dogs

*(I know plenty of poems about dogs but this is the only one I ever
wrote for a dog, a golden retriever called Polly. She liked to listen
to it while her chest was being tickled. Try it on a dog you love,
changing the name of course, and reciting it over and over in a*

gentle, deep voice. You will find that most dogs enjoy this game,
especially after supper.)

Good Polly
Good dog.
Good Polly,
Good dog.

For Number Ten

One out of ten, six gold, four black.
Born in a bulging, transparent sack.

I eased him out, this holy gift.
His mother turned to him and sniffed

Then licked the blood and the sack away.
All small and golden, there he lay.

There are some insects and some flowers
Whose life is spent in twenty-four hours.

For twenty-four hours, beside his mother,
He fed and he slept with his sisters and brothers.

Umpteen Pockets

Good smells. Close warm. Then a crushing weight.
Then nothing at all. His head the wrong shape.

He was wrapped up and taken beyond the bounds
Of his mother's familiar digging grounds

For she would have found him and known him too
And have wept as golden retrievers do.

So she kept all her love for the alive –
The black four and the golden five.

But I celebrate that golden pup
Whom I talked to and kissed as I wrapped him up.

For he fed and he slept and was loved as he lay
In the dark where he spent one golden day.

Now his mother pursues an eccentric trail
With casual sweeps of her lavish gold tail

And when number ten stumbles into my mind
She consoles me and so do the other nine

Adrian Mitchell

Epitaph For A Golden Retriever

It was my job
To be a dog

My master said
That I was good

Now I turn myself around
And lie down in the musky ground

A Cat Called Slumber

In the middle of the night appears
My day-shy tabby with collapsible ears
And I stroke her head so those ears collapse
And she purrs to say that she loves me, perhaps

My Cat Slumber Speaks Of Celia

At five in the morning when my human is asleep
I stalk on to her eiderdown and crouch on her
Oh she's a warm and friendly-smelling heap
So I purr and I purr and I purr.

Iceberg Academy

the only floating shipwrecked school
in the known universe

Five Years Old

Five-year-olds dream of becoming giants –
Golden-bearded, striding around the map,
Gulping streams, munching sandwiches
Of crushed ice and white-hot anthracite
Between two slices of slate.
They sit on the edge of Salisbury Plain
Bawling huge songs across the counties
For ten days at a time,
Eating trees, cuddling carthorses,
Before stomping home to Windsor Castle.
They name clouds. They fall in love with buses,
They lick the stars, they are amazed by hoses,
They dance all the time because they don't think about
dancing...

They long to be allowed into the big good schools
Which will teach them to be giants with wings.

Adrian Mitchell

Amazing Mathematical Discovery Rocks Universe Essex Man Slightly Hurt

Nobel Maths Wizards Make Odd Discovery –
Two Plus Two Has Stopped Making Four.

TWO PLUS TWO MAKES FIVE AND A BIT!

Schoolkids Burn Dummies of Einstein and Newton,
Those old dummies, as they chant:
Two Plus Two Makes Five And A Bit!

Their faulty arithmetic finally exposed –
Suspension bridges go haywire!
Skyscrapers sway, fold and collapse into their own cellars!
Cash registers, calculators and computers
Short-circuit themselves in mass suicide.
The Thames fills up with stockbrokers and Vatmen!
Only the average people
Whose maths is so far below average
Go about their normal unbusinesslike business –
Making things without measuring them exactly,
Only pretending to count the change,
Buying Two and Two
And being charged Five And A Bit.

The Secret Number Burrow

Only its whiskers showed above the ground.
Its squat head and odd-sided body were covered
By the deep dust. I reached down and found
The scruff of its skull, pulled it up. I'd discovered
The number which hides between Eight and Nine.
It is called *Shtoogeree*. It is mine. All mine.

Adrian Mitchell

Two-Minute Girl

(In some schools, two minutes before classes start,
a Two-Minute Girl or Boy pokes his or her head round
the Staffroom door and warns the teachers to Get Ready)

I'm the Two-Minute Girl
I'm about the size of a briefcase
I have bunches done up with barbed wire
And Count Dracula pointy teeth

I'm the Two-Minute Girl
I'm as sweet as syrup pudding on the surface
But I'm as wicked as stinging nettles underneath

Two minutes early or two minutes late
I stick my head round the staffroom door
And sometimes I whisper like the ghost of a snake
(two minutes) and leave the teachers to snore

Yes I'm the Two-Minute Girl
I'm as cunning as cunning can be
With the driving brain of a diesel train
And the mischieviousness of a flea

Oh I'm the Two-Minute Girl
I love to spread the Two-Minute Blues
Especially when I bellow TWO MINUTES!
And a teacher pours the teapot all over his new suede shoes

Lost Love Poem

One day they'll manufacture eggs,
The formula for snowflakes will be clear
And love explained – that's not the day
I think about, the day I marked on my calendar.

Because they appreciate their legs,
Simple creatures will career
Through boundless grass. One day, the day
I think about, the day I marked on my calendar.

In the classroom the boy with ragged fingernails
Flicks a note to the girl whose hair solidifies
All the light there is. The note says:
Some day, when I'm grown up, some day –
It falls between the floorboards...

The Blackboard

Five foot by five foot
(The smalls have measured it).
Smooth black surface
(Wiped by a small after every class).
Five different colours of chalk
And a class of twenty-five smalls,
One big.
Does the big break up the chalk
Into twenty-five or twenty-six
And invite the smalls to make
A firework show of colours
Shapes and words
Starting on the blackboard

But soon overflowing
All over the room
  All over the school
    All over the town
      All over the country
        All over the world?

  No.

The big looks at the textbook
Which was written by a big
And published by a firm of bigs.
The textbook says
The names and dates of Nelson's battles.
So the big writes, in white,
Upon the black of the blackboard,
The names and dates of Nelson's battles.
The smalls copy into their books
The names and dates of Nelson's battles.

    Nelson was a big
Who died fighting for freedom or something.

Adrian Mitchell

Teachers Are Not Allowed To Take Their Clothes Off

This is a new rule
It was not thought necessary
But a new teacher came to school
There she was in the staffroom with nothing on
The School Secretary said to her
You were wearing clothes when we interviewed you
Yes said the new nude teacher
But I was so pleased to get a job
That I went home and took off my clothes
And my cats took one look at me
And started to sing and dance
So I burned all my clothes
And I feel much better.
This is the reason for the new rule.

School Dinners

Lumpy custard and liver – ugh!
I hate school dinners and I'll tell you why.
There's dog food with peas in, there's Secret Stew,
And a cheese and bacon thing we call Sick Pie.

Back In The Playground Blues

I dreamed I was back in the playground, I was about four feet high
Yes dreamed I was back in the playground, standing about four
     feet high
Well the playground was three miles long and the playground was
     five miles wide

It was broken black tarmac with a high wire fence all around
Broken black dusty tarmac with a high fence running all around
And it had a special name to it, they called it The Killing Ground

Got a mother and a father, they're one thousand years away
The rulers of The Killing Ground are coming out to play
Everybody thinking: "Who they going to play with today?"

    Well you get it for being Jewish
    And you get it for being black
    Get it for being chicken
    And you get it for fighting back
    You get it for being big and fat
    Get it for being small
    Oh those who get it get it and get it
    For any damn thing at all

Sometimes they take a beetle, tear off its six legs one by one
Beetle on its black back, rocking in the lunchtime sun
But a beetle can't beg for mercy, a beetle's not half the fun

I heard a deep voice talking, it had that iceberg sound
"It prepares them for Life" – but I have never found
Any place in my life worse than The Killing Ground.

Elephantasia

an island of assorted animals
ruled over by a wise and
cheerful herd of tuskers

Adrian Mitchell

Nature Poem

Skylark, what prompts your silver song
To fountain up and down the sky?

Beetles roast
With fleas on toast
And earthworm pie.

Yorkshire Epitaph

he could run right fast
a ginger-golden hump of fur
but his retractable feet could move over the Yorkshire grass
so we called him after the best runner we could remember
     Zatopec
          after a night of frost
          found dead in his netted house
          legs straight out
          a dark stain round his mouth
          a globe tear in the corner of one eye
          he was buried in the flower bed
            Zatopec, our lone guinea pig
          he could run right fast

Not A Very Cheerful Song, I'm Afraid

There was a gloomy lady,
With a gloomy duck and a gloomy drake,
And they all three wandered gloomily,
Beside a gloomy lake,
On a gloomy, gloomy, gloomy, gloomy, gloomy, gloomy day.

Now underneath that gloomy lake
The gloomy lady's gone.
But the gloomy duck and the gloomy drake
Swim on and on and on,
On a gloomy, gloomy, gloomy, gloomy, gloomy, gloomy day.

Rat It Up

C'mon everybody
Slap some grease on those paws
Get some yellow on your teeth
And, uh, sharpen up your claws

There's a whole lot of sausage
We're gonna swallow down
We're gonna jump out the sewers
And rock this town

Cos we're ratting it up
Yes we're ratting it up
Well we're ratting it up
For a ratting good time tonight

Ain't got no compass
You don't need no map
Just follow your snout
Hey, watch out for that trap!

Umpteen Pockets

You can take out a poodle
You can beat up a cat
But if you can't lick a ferret
You ain't no kind of rat

    Cos we're ratting it up
    Yes we're ratting it up
    Well we're ratting it up
    For a ratting good time tonight

Now you can sneak in the henhouse
Roll out the eggs
But if the farmer comes running
Bite his hairy legs

Check that cheese for poison
Before you eat
Or you'll wind up being served up
As ratburger meat

    Cos we're ratting it up
    Yes we're ratting it up
    Well we're ratting it up
    For a ratting good time tonight

Adrian Mitchell

This rat was born to rock
This rat was born to roll
I don't give a monkey's
Bout your pest control

So push off pussy-cat
Push off pup
We're the Rockin' Rodents
And we're ratting it up

Yeah we're ratting it up
Yeah we're ratting it up
Well we're ratting it up
For a ratting good time tonight!

Hog In A Wood

Big black hog in a wood
On a truffle hunt.
Head stuck deep in the earth –
Grunt, snort, grunt.

Oh a hog's in heaven when his tongue
Is wrapped around a truffle.
His tail uncurls and his hog heart
Performs a soft-shoe shuffle.

Big black hog in a wood
Chewing muddy truffles.
Great snout nosing them out –
Sniff, snuff, snuffles.

Adrian Mitchell

Understanding The Rain

(for a horse called Elgin)

Top right-hand corner
Of a South Devon field
The great white horse
Stands under the warm rain

Slow-motion grass
Growing greener and greener
The great white horse
Stands under the warm rain

Like a shining cathedral
Under the centuries
The great white horse
Stands under the warm rain

Like a waiting messenger
Like the people of England
Like the planet Earth
Like poetry
Like a great white horse
The great white horse
Stands under the warm rain

Never Forget The Birthday Of Anyone Who Has Antlers Bigger Than Your Body

No excuse
Is any use
To a deeply offended Moose

Cookery Advice

If stuck in a kitchen
With a hungry leopard
Ask him: Would you like me
Salted and peppered?

Revenge

The elephant knocked the ground with a stick,
He knocked it slow, he knocked it quick.
He knocked it till his trunk turned black –
Then the ground turned round and knocked him back.

The Galactic Pachyderm

The elephant stands
        among the stars
He jumps off
        Neptune
bounces off
        Mars
to adventures on
        Venus
while his children
        play
in the diamond jungles
        of the
Milky Way

Tinkling The Ivories

There was an elephant
    called Art Tatum
He played a piano
    whose keys were human teeth

Non-Event

If an elephant could meet a whale
their understanding would be huge
and they would love one another for ever

Adrian Mitchell

Pride

The elephant
is not proud of being an elephant
So why are we ashamed?

Good Taste

The vilest furniture in this land
is an elephant's foot umbrella stand

Love Poem, Elephant Poem

Elephants are as amazing as love
but love is as amazing as elephants
Love is as amazing as elephants
but elephants are as amazing as love

You Aren't What You Eat

The elephant
who's seldom flustered
despises calming food
like custard
Devouring curry
in a hurry
washed down with
a mug of mustard

Adrian Mitchell

The Infant Elephant Speaks:

I got a rusk
stuck on my tusk

Turn Turn Turn

There is a time for considering elephants
There is no time for not considering elephants

Elephant Eternity

Elephants walking under juicy-leaf trees
Walking with their children under juicy-leaf trees
Elephants elephants walking like time

Elephants bathing in the foam-floody river
Fountaining their children in the mothery river
Elephants elephants bathing like happiness

    Strong and gentle elephants
    Standing on the earth
    Strong and gentle elephants
    Like peace

Time is walking under elephant trees
Happiness is bathing in the elephant river
Strong gentle peace is shining
All over the elephant earth

spookalulu

where there are heroes on
the purple hills and monsters
lurking in the chilly caves

Third Time Unlucky

ghosts playing dice
with dice made of ice
they let you win once
they let you win twice

Official Notice

Persons with Dogs or Chimpanzees:
Try to distract their attention, please,
When promenading past the Giant Cheese.

Adrian Mitchell

Golo, The Gloomy Goalkeeper

Golo plays for the greatest soccer team in the Universe.
They are so mighty that their opponents never venture out
        of their own penalty area.
They are so all-conquering that Golo never touches the ball
        during a match, and very seldom sees it.
Every game seems to last a lifetime to Golo,
        the Gloomy Goalkeeper.

Golo scratches white paint off the goalposts' surface to reveal
        the silver shining underneath.
He kisses the silver of the goalpost.
It does not respond.

He counts the small stones in the penalty area.
There are three hundred and seventy eight, which is not
        his lucky number.
Golo pretends to have the hiccups, then says to himself,
        imitating his sister's voice:
Don't breathe, and just die basically.

He breaks eight small sticks in half.
Then he has sixteen very small sticks.
He plants geranium seeds along the goal-line.
He paints a picture of a banana and sells it to the referee
      at half-time.

Golo finds, among the bootmarks in the dust, the print of
      one stiletto heel.
He crawls around on all fours doing lion imitations.
He tries to read his future in the palm of his hand, but
      forgets to take his glove off.
He writes a great poem about butterflies but tears it up
      because he can't think of a rhyme for Wednesday.
He knits a sweater for the camel in the zoo.

Golo suddenly realises he can't remember if he is a man
      or a woman.
He takes a quick look, but still can't decide.

He makes up his mind that grass is his favourite colour.
He puts on boots, track-suit, gloves and hat all the same
      colour as grass.
He paints his face a gentle shade of green.

He lies down on the pitch and becomes invisible.
The grass tickles the back of his neck.
At last Golo is happy.
He has fallen in love with the grass.
And the grass has fallen in love with Golo,
    the Gloomy Goalkeeper.

Unlucky Steps

Thirteen steps
Leading me down
Down to that big blue door
Big blue door
With a grime-lined face
And a voice like a polar bear roar,
The sound of a mechanized blizzard
Which froze my trainers to the floor.

It sounded like a cloud of poison gas
Whispering evil to itself.
It sounded like a bunch of defrosting cobras
Slithering off their shelf.

I pushed down the handle
The handle stayed down
For three point five seconds at least
Then the handle sprang back
And the wild white sound
Of a beast that longed to be released
Suddenly stopped.

Adrian Mitchell

The silence swelled and swelled and swelled
As if it were about to burst.
My heart felt like a blue iced lolly
    On an ice rink
      In Alaska
        On December the 21st.

I backed up the steps
    13, 12, 11
Away from the cupboard of snows
I backed up the steps
    10, 9, 8, 7
I don't want to join the Eskimos
I backed up the steps
    6, 5, 4
My heart saying: Go man, go man!
I backed up the steps
Then I turned around –
That's when I got eaten by a Snowman.

The Set-Square, Square-Set Gunman
(for geometricians and Country and Western fans)

I come from Euclid County, where the savage Cosines ride
And under the Geomma Tree I tunes my old guitar.
My pappy was a Cube who took a Spiral fer his bride
So I wuz born to be rectangular.

Yup. Both my sides is parallel and I'm broader than I'm high,
But have no doubt about my shoot-it-out capacity,
Fer I've got more angles than Isosceles, plus a Pythagorean eye
And all the cowpokes call me Oblong Cassidy.

The Floating Flautist

I wish I lived in a house in the clouds:
I'd serenade wing-clapping seagull crowds.
My flute would purr and ripple and trill
And angels would perch on my window-sill.

Their Voices

One had a voice like an ancient wooden desk
Initials cut deep all over
And then inked in, black, blue and blue-black.

Two had a voice like a rubbish dump –
Old cabbages tumbling out of a sack.

Three had a voice like a fountain on a mountain
And a holiday stream bounding down the rocks.

Four had a voice like a willow-tree.

Five had a voice like a jack-in-the-box.

But what did they say? What decisions were made?
Dunno. I only listened to the music they played.

I Am Boj

(to be shouted, in the voice of a terrible giant,
at children who wake early).

I am Boj

I crackle like the Wig of a Judge

I am Boj

My eyes boil over with Hodge-Podge

I am Boj

Organised Sludge and a Thunder-Wedge

I am Boj

I am a Tower of solid Grudge

I am Boj

The molten Centre, the cutting Edge

I am Boj

From deepest Dudgeon I swing my Bludgeon

I am Boj

Adrian Mitchell

Giving Potatoes

Strong Man:
Mashed potatoes cannot hurt you, darling
Mashed potatoes mean no harm
I have brought you mashed potatoes
From my mashed potato farm.

Lady:
Take away your mashed potatoes
Leave them in the desert to dry
Take away your mashed potatoes –
You look like shepherd's pie.

Brash Man:
A packet of chips, a packet of chips,
Wrapped in the Daily Mail,
Golden and juicy and fried for a week
In the blubber of the Great White Whale.

Lady:
Take away your fried potatoes
Use them to clean your ears
You can eat your fried potatoes
With Birds-Eye frozen tears.

Old Man:
I have borne this baked potato
O'er the Generation Gap,
Pray accept this baked potato
Let me lay it in your heated lap.

Lady:
Take away your baked potato
In your fusty musty van
Take away your baked potato
You potato-skinned old man.

Frenchman:
She rejected all potatoes
For a thousand night and days
Till a Frenchman wooed and won her
With pommes de terre Lyonnaises.

Lady:
Oh my corrugated lover
So creamy and so brown
Let us fly across to Lyons
And lay our tubers down.

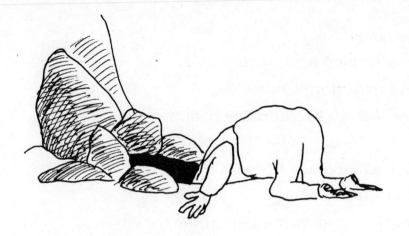

What's That Down There?

What's that down there?
What's that moving?
What's that moving down in the dark
                of this chilly black maze of a cave?

Is it Sarallo –
The scarlet snake with the seven
Silver heads
And fangs that snap like a murder trap?

What's that down there?
What's that moving?
What's that moving down in the dark
                of this chilly black maze of a cave?

Umpteen Pockets

Is it Farranaway –
That back-cracking brute
With a hundred horns
And hoofs that hit like horrible hammers?

What's that down there?
What's that moving?
What's that moving down in the dark
of this chilly black maze of a cave?

Is it Thilissa –
That slippery wisp of
A whispering ghost of a
Girl who died
In the moistness of mist
Which lies like a shroud on
The underground lake
down in the dark in this chilly black maze of a cave?

Adrian Mitchell

The Gondoliers of Greenland

The Gondoliers of Greenland
Are the Grumpiest folk in the North
Their canals melt on August the Second
And freeze up on August the Fourth.
In those two laborious glorious days
All their incomes must be made
And the rest of the year they wait listlessly
To ply their ridiculous trade.

Balloon Lagoon

in whose blue waters you
may see reflected views
of the strange Planet Earth

Adrian Mitchell

Song In Space

When man first flew beyond the sky
He looked back into the world's blue eye.
Man said: What makes your eye so blue?
Earth said: The tears in the ocean do.
Why are the seas so full of tears?
Because I've wept so many thousand years.
Why do you weep as you dance through space?
Because I am the Mother of the Human Race.

Keep Your Airplanes
Away From Our Islands

the islands of Toronto
sleep upon the waters

small grass and friendly trees
are talking to the giant sky

a garter snake whispers across the path
the tyres of a bicycle whisper back

you can hear my brother singing to his boots
a squeaky song about the olden days
as the swing creaks him up to the sun

my mother plays the flute and her music makes
a fountain of birds fountain over the waters

you can hear so much on these lovely islands
which rose from the lake in an age of silence

you can hear the breathing of your best friend
you can hear the blood swimming around your veins

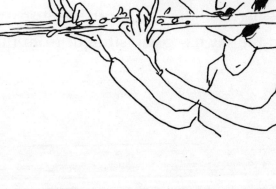

you can hear a slow and barefoot tread
which I believe is the sound of peace walking

peace upon the islands
peace upon the waters

as the islands of Toronto
sleep on the holy waters

Thankful For A Rainfall

A Pyrenean Mountain Dog
Sprawls on a sofa

An early, furry mist
Lies all along the river

Two trees lean against a third
Still discussing last year's storm

Last night's rain has travelled up to London
Blobs from the rim of my hut remember him

Sunshine tickles
The thankful thistles

Butterflies stumble around the breeze
Cats tip-toe among brand-new puddles

Blessings roll down the earth's dusty red throat
And the sky has come straight from the washing machine

Adrian Mitchell

The Mighty Man
On The Mower

In my soft and silver helmet
I ride across the plain
For I am proud and supple
And happy as the moon.

My chariot was made of steel
For Saladin the Saracen.
It is drawn by a dragon
Whose roaring mouth spouts flames of green...

The Big Fall

I'm a leaf that came to grief, chief,
Fell off that good old tree,
Flittered and fluttered down to the ground –
Why did it have to be meedle-e-dee
Why did it have to be me?

I was happy as a humbug in my good old tree
But now I'm all flopsome and lost.
I get all soggy in the thumpering rain
And I crinkle like a cornflake in the frost.
O yes, I crunkle like a flornflake in the frost.

So carry me away to the compost heap
With ten thousand other loose leaves like me.
I'll be happy as a hamster in the compost heap
Dreaming of my good old treedle-e-dee
Dreaming of my good old tree.

Winter Listening

Humble, crumbly song of the snails.
Pinecones rattling in a stormy tree.
The frosty voices of December stars.
Dragon-roaring of a scarlet factory.

Honking slapstick of seals at play.
The creak and slish of snow off a roof.
Crackle-whisper of Christmas paper.
The silver step of a unicorn's hoof.

Winter Bully

Somebody beat up November the Tenth –
(Maybe December the First) –
It wore a sky like a black eye
And was crying fit to burst.

Round and Round

The handle swings the mallet
The mallet drives the wedge
The wedge cracks the tree trunk
With its cutting edge
The chainsaw comes roaring in to fell it
Then a carpenter takes a slice of the tree
And carves out the handle for a mallet

Adrian Mitchell

A Speck Speaks

About ten million years ago
I was a speck of rock in a vast black rock.
My address was:

      Vast Black Rock,

      Near Italy,

      Twelve Metres Under

The Mediterranean Sea.

The other specks and I
Formed an impressive edifice –
Bulbously curving at the base
With rounded caves
And fun tunnels for the fish,
Romantically jagged at the top.

Life, for us specks, was uneventful –
One for all, welded together
In the cool, salty wet.
What more could specks
Expect?
Each year a few of us were lost,
Scrubbed from the edges of the rock
By the washerwoman waters

Which smoothed our base, whittled our cornices
And sharpened our pinnacles.
As the rock slowly shed skin-thin layers
It was my turn to be exposed
Among the packed grit of its surface,
(Near the tip of the fifty-ninth spire
From the end of the eastern outcrop).

One day, it was a Wednesday I remember,
A scampi flicked me off my perch
Near the vast black rock's peak
And I was scurried down
Long corridors of currents
Until a wave caught me in its mouth
And spat me out on –
What?
A drying stretch
Of yellow, white, black, red and transparent specks,
Billions of particles,
Loosely organized in bumps and dips;
Quite unlike the tight hard group
Which I belonged to in the good old rock.
Heat banged down on us all day long.
Us? I turned to the speck next to me,
 A lumpish red fellow who'd been washed off a brick.

"I'm new here," I confessed,
"What are we supposed to be?"
He bellowed back –
(But the bellow of a speck
Is less than the whispering of ants) –
"We're grains now, grains of sand,
And this society is called Beach."

"Beach?" I said. "What are we grains supposed to do?"
"Just stray around, lie loose,
Go with the wind, go with the sea
And sink down when you're trodden on."
"Don't know if I can manage that.
Used to belong to Vast Black Rock
And we all stuck together."

"Give Beach a try," said the red grain.
Well, there was no alternative.

Many eras later
I was just beginning to feel
Part of Beach, that slow-drifting,
Slow-shifting, casual community,
When I was shovelled up
With a ton of fellow grains,

Umpteen Pockets

Hoisted into a lorry, shaken down a road,
Washed, sifted and poured in a machine
Hotter than the sunshine.

When they poured me out, life had changed again.
My mates and I swam in a molten river
Down into a mould.
White-hot we were, then red, then
Suddenly cold
And we found ourselves merged
Into a tall, circular tower,
Wide at the bottom, narrow at the top
What's more, we'd all turned green as sea-weed.
Tranparent green.
We had become – a wine bottle.

In a few flashes of time
We'd been filled with wine,
Stoppered, labelled, bumped to a shop,
Stood in a window, sold, refrigerated,
Drained by English tourists,
Transmogrified into a lampstand,
Smashed by a four-year-old called Tarquin,
Swept up, chucked in the garbage, hauled away,
Dumped and bulldozed into the sea.

Adrian Mitchell

Now the underwater years sandpaper away
My shield-shaped fragment of bottle.
So one day I shall be a single grain again,
A single grain of green, transparent glass.

When that day comes
I will transmit a sub-aquatic call
To all green specks of glass
Proposing that we form
A Vast Green Rock of Glass,
Near Italy,
Twelve Metres Under
The Mediterranean Sea.

Should be pretty spectacular
In about ten million years.

All being well.

A Child Is Singing

A child is singing
And nobody listening
But the child who is singing:

Bulldozers grab the earth and shower it.
    The house is on fire.
Gardeners wet the earth and flower it.
    The house is on fire.
    The houses are on fire.
Fetch the fire engine, the fire engine's on fire.
    We will have to hide in a hole.
    We will burn slow, like coal.
    All the people are on fire.

And a child is singing
And nobody listening
But the child who is singing.

A Valentine Poem

For Cathy Pompe's Kids
at St Paul's Primary School, Cambridge
(who were about 6 – 7 years old)

The night is a dark blue balloon
The day is a golden balloon
The moon longs to cuddle the sun
The sun longs to cuddle the moon

Index of first lines

Daft as a Doughnut

DAFT AS A DOUGHNUT

CONTENTS

ALL AROUND THE WORLD

MAGIC JOURNEYS

DAFT AS A DOUGHNUT

POETRY D.I.Y.

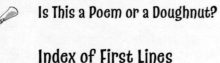

Come On In

Daft as a Doughnut

Happy as a holiday
Grumpy as a grown-up
Potty as a poet's day
Daft as a doughnut

Bloated as a big balloon
When it's being blown up
Jazzy as a jungle moon

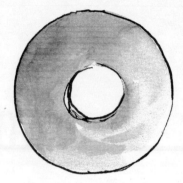

Daft as a doughnut

Adrian Mitchell

How to Write Poems

Bite your lower lip,

Stick out your tongue.

That's the way

The poems get done.

Screw up your eyes,

Take a new look.

That's the way

Poems start to cook.

265

A Poet's Life for Me

"Are you the Author Dude?" – small American boy
just before my poetry performance in Seattle.

I was born wearing jeans and an invisible hat,
With the heart of a mouse but the rhythm of a cat.

At eight I stowed away on a pirate vessel
Sailing over the Ocean of Dreams
And there I was taught how to write, rhyme and wrestle
By a mermaid selling hot ice-creams.

Adrian Mitchell

At eighteen I was a tramp in the City of Trees
And studied in a College of Chimpanzees.
I learned How To Dance The Banana Fling,
How To Doze On A Branch and How To Swing.

But now I run a Poetry Corner Shop
Selling Fizzy Crisps and Cheese And Onion Pop,
And I write for kisses and I write for kicks –
So come on in – mix and match and pick and mix!

Adrian Mitchell

My Favourite Word

My favourite word is Animals –
The plural, not the singular,
For in that one word Animals,
How many miracles there are.

Mrs Christmas

She was about as small as a cup
But big as your head when she grew up
And she came to stay on Christmas Day
So we called her Mrs Christmas

She liked to swoop around the hall
With a silver paper soccer ball
And I think I was four but maybe some more
When I named her Mrs Christmas

She had some kittens with bright white socks
And she kept them in a brown cardboard box
And she'd nudge them out and march them about
Saying:

"I am Mrs Christmas"

Adrian Mitchell

Dog Bog

I know a dog
His name is Josh
In the muddy muddy bog
Josh likes to splosh
When I say Josh
You need a wash
He says By gosh
I don't want to be posh
I want to splosh splosh splosh
In the muddy muddy bog
All day

I know a dog
Her name is Trish
In the muddy muddy bog
Trish likes to splish
When I say Trish
You're not a fish
She says Oh pish
It's my only wish
I want to splish splish splish
In the muddy muddy bog
All day

Umpteen Pockets

I know a dog
Her name is Sash
In the muddy muddy bog
Sash likes to splash
When I say Sash
The bog's full of trash
She says Balderdash
It's a lovely mish-mash
I want to splash splash splash
In the muddy muddy bog
All day

splosh splosh splosh goes my friend Josh
splish splish splish goes my friend Trish
splash splash splash goes my friend Sash
splash   splish   splosh
In the muddy muddy bog
All day

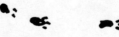

Adrian Mitchell

Disguise

Every morning after I shampoo my fur
I climb into my humanskin costume and
Put on my human mask and human clothes
Then I go out into the human city
And catch a human bus to work

As I sit at my computer
Summoning up images of the
    financial world
None of my colleagues know
That inside my human hand gloves
Are the brown and burly
Sharp and curly
Paws of a grizzly bear

Yes, I am a bear in a cunning disguise,
Only passing as human
Trying not to yield to temptation
As I lumber past
The sticky buns in the baker's shop
The honeycombs in the health shop

Umpteen Pockets

I am married to a human woman who knows my secret
We have a human daughter
Who is rather furry and has deep golden eyes
And gentle paws
We call her Bruinhilda

I took Bruinhilda to a circus once
But there was a performing bear
Riding a unicycle, juggling with flames
Dancing to an accordion

I sat tight
Though she might have been my mother
I sat tight
While the inside of my human mask
Filled up with the tears of a bear

Adrian Mitchell

There's No Business Like Slow Business

A Snail named Maurice
met a Slug called Doris

off to the forest
crawled Maurice and Doris

to watch a show
by Boris the Slow
Loris
for Maurice and Doris
love Boris the Loris

he's funny
he's furry
and he's **SO**

slooooooooooooow

The Pelican

The sunset glows
Like the inside of a peach
I see a pelican
Standing on the beach
The pelican looks
So clumsy and sad
I want to take him home
To my mum and dad
But he shakes his long beak
And jumps into the skies

And graceful as an angel Away he flies

Gorillas

Moonlight upon the mountains
And the gentle Gorillas awake

They lumber along through the forest
To sit by the side of the lake

And there in the silvery water
They dangle their ticklish toes

And what the Gorillas are thinking
Nobody nobody knows

The Arrival of the Seal

Tailfin churning like an outboard motor
He charges through the ice floe and up the shore
He toots for his mate with his boot-polished hooter
And a million diamonds shine all over his fur

Nobody Rides
the Unicorn

His coat is like snowflakes
Woven with silk.
When he goes galloping
He flows like milk.

His life is all gentle
And his heart is bold.
His single horn is magical
Barley sugar gold.

Nobody rides the Unicorn
As he grazes under a secret sun.
His understanding is so great
That he forgives us, every one.

Nobody rides the Unicorn,
His mind is peaceful as the grass.
He is the loveliest one of all
And he sleeps behind the waterfall.

Adrian Mitchell

To See a Unicorn

This is the way to see a Unicorn:

Close your eyes.

See a sandy path in front of you.
Follow that path over a hill of grass and daisies.

Take a deep breath.
See a bumpy little stream in front of you.

Follow that stream into a forest.
Take a deep breath.

See a clearing in the forest
And a pool like a mirror for the trees.

Take a deep breath.
Be still.

Umpteen Pockets

Who walks so gracefully down to the pool
And bends to drink the cool dark water?

It is the Unicorn, the loveliest of animals.
He loves to wander in the forest of your dreams.

See his silver mane and his golden horn
See his gentle eyes.
Hear the beating of his heart.

Be still.

Open your eyes
When you want to open your eyes.

Remember the Unicorn.

Adrian Mitchell

Welcoming the Birds

You hold up your hand.

Now your hand's a tree.

Small birds fly to it

Gratefully

And they rest their wings,

Your sweet-singing friends,

As they perch like snowflakes

On your fingers' ends.

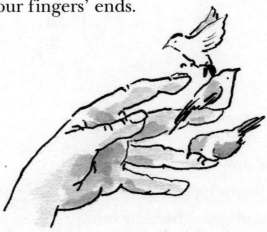

Henry the Golden Retriever

Ten months old
Same colour as the sunshine

Over the grass he jumps

His only fault
Is bumping into you
But they are friendly bumps

Adrian Mitchell

All the Animals Gathered Round

Guitar in his hand
Leaning on an Elephant
Orpheus sings

A Wolfhound and St Bernard
At his knees

A grey Ox
Cocks his ear

Two Swans
Lift their snaking heads
Towards the music

The Geese are paddling in the shadows
Gathering peppery green weeds

A flowering Ostrich on a rock
Throws back her wings
In ecstasy

The Waterfall bounces
Silver notes

A Leopard reclining
Like a streamlined blonde

A Lion and Lioness
Roll their golden eyes

A Heron taking off
On a journey to the hidden stars

The Peacock flaunts
His starry blue
Waterfall of a tail

A million Birds
In proud mid-flight
Scattering their colours
All over the sky

A lurking Buffalo
With guilty eyes

Adrian Mitchell

A family of Deer
Guarding each other with their branches

Birds and Animals
Feeding   Drinking   Singing   Resting

The Trees are dancing
Stretching and swirling
And the Sky is a dance
Of speeding blue and white

It is all a dance
And at its centre
The wedding of two Horses
They have a special temple
Of grass and flowers
Among the shining rocks

The Grey Horse looks at us
The Chestnut turns away
Their flanks are touching
Silver flank against
Chestnut flank

Two Horses
So glad and close together
It can only be love

Never lose it

Guitar in his hands
Leaning on an Elephant
Orpheus sings

(Orpheus was such a great singer that when he sang all the animals, both wild and tame, gathered round him. This poem is a description of a beautiful painting, by Roelant Savery, in the Fitzwilliam Museum, Cambridge. It's a very small, bright, crowded picture and you have to look carefully to find Orpheus and the Elephant up in the top right-hand corner.)

Adrian Mitchell

Gubblefish Soup

Take a one-eyed frog
From a bubbling bog
Rub him down with talcum powder
Feed a kidney cake
To a rattlesnake
And then pound him into chowder
Pour them in a dish
With some jellyfish
Boil them up till they're delicious
Don't be cautious
Add a pair of galoshes
And a bunch of gubblefishes

Gubblefish gubblefish gubblefish soup
Your eyebrows jump
Your whiskers droop
Your guts go boing!
And you loop the loop
With gubblefish gubblefish gubblefish soup

Take a dozen pails
Full of giant snails
And a fried Egyptian mummy
Melt a telescope
With a bar of soap
That'll make the mixture yummy
Stir 'em up with glue
To a steamy stew
And squash 'em till they squishes
That's a jumbo
Kind of mumbo gumbo
And it tastes like – gubblefishes

Gubblefish gubblefish gubblefish soup
Your eyebrows jump
Your whiskers droop
Your guts go boing!
And you loop the loop
With gubblefish gubblefish gubblefish soup

Adrian Mitchell

Fights I Have Fighted

When I fought a Boa Constrictor –
I licked 'er.

In a battle with a Cheetah –

I easily beat her.

But when I saw an Axolotl –

I lost me bottle.

Electric Advice

Never take
A bath in the dark.
You might use the wrong flannel

or sit on a shark.

Only Kidding

Sticky-up Hair

I've got sticky-up hair
I've got sticky-up hair
Like a tuft of grass
On top of a hillock.

I've got sticky-out teeth
I've got sticky-out teeth
But they don't make me
Look like a pillock.

Doing the Best I Can

Dad
showed me
my new
half-sister.

I love Dad
so I
half-kissed her.

Adrian Mitchell

Just Me

My name is Benjy
I am three
I want to walk downstairs –
    Just me.

Out in the street
I want to be
I'll catch a bus –
    Just me.

I'll drive that bus
Over the sea
To a magic island –
    Just me.

I'll live in a hut
In a monkey tree
Eating chocolate parrots –
    Just me.

Umpteen Pockets

Then I'll make a plane
And fly off to see
The African Jungle –
    Just me.

I'll meet an elephant
Called Tennessee.
I'll ride on his back –
    Just me.

He'll carry me home
Across the sea.
I'll shout: "I'm back
    With Tennessee!"

Adrian Mitchell

We'll drink a mug
Of elephant tea,
Then we'll clump upstairs –
Tennessee and me.

He can sleep
In the lower bunk
So I can reach down
    To pat his trunk.

And I'll tell him about
How it used to be
When I had no elephant friend –
Just me.

It Came from Under the Table

It came from under the table
During one of Grandpa's speeches.
We heard its movements down below
Like the squelch of rotten peaches.

It came from under the table
With the scent of forgotten cheese
But first it chewed on our toenails
And then it nibbled our knees.

O its clammy touch
Was much too much –
Father dashed off to work
Gran hid herself
On the teapot shelf
And the rest of them went berserk.

Yes it came from under the table
Like a phantom from the sea.
But I was the scaredest one of all –

Was I It? Or was It me?

Adrian Mitchell

To Caitlin Riding on my Shoulders

When you're up there
High in the air
Riding upon my shoulder
You play with my hair
Like it's some kind of rare
White grass growing
On an old pink boulder

Don't you know I'm underneath
With my detachable teeth
Thinking how wonderfully wild you are
So hang on tight
Pull my scalp off that's all right
Your ever-loving Grandpapa

In Mrs Moon's Class

I write words down on paper
I fit them in between the lines
The paper is white
The lines are light blue

Straight rivers in rows
On oblong fields of snow

I look up at the blackboard
Wide night sky
With a few white speck stars

My teacher's face is the moon
The moon is white
The moon is very far away

I do not know what the moon
   thinks
The moon is bright
The moon does not know
   what I think so

I write words down on paper

Sunset Verse

The setting sun is like an orange
Writes our poetic teacher, Lucy.
So where's the pips, yells Billy Cripps,
Why isn't the sun juicy?

A NOTICE TO STICK
UP ON THE DOOR
OF YOUR ROOM

If Sneaky-Snoop
Comes sniffing around
Something really horrible
Will always be found

The Sadness of
a Giant Child

I'm four years old.
I'm eight feet high.
They take me to a little school
And leave me to cry.

The grown-ups laugh.
The children scream.
I feel like a hairy
Monster in a dream.

Our teacher is a Tiny.
We call her Miss Priscilla.
Her favourite fairy story
Is Jack the Giant-Killer.

I sit in the corner
Like a wardrobe to sulk.
The other kids call me
The Inedible Hulk

And the only time they let me
Join in a game
Is when I let them use me
As a climbing frame.

So each night I pray
To the God of the Tall:
"Please, Lord, let me
Grow up to be small."

Lighting Up Time

you're afraid of the dark
you try to be brave
you screw up your eyes
so you can't see the dark

but you can still feel
how the dark fills your room
you can still feel
the dark on your face
and you're afraid of the dark

don't be afraid
I will stand beside your bed
and hold up both my hands
and stretch my fingers
and each finger shall be
a bright-dancing candle
filling your room with gentle light

Adrian Mitchell

so don't be afraid of the dark
and I'll stand by your bed
to shine away the dark
every night until you say
go away now go away
I'm not afraid of the dark any more

Little Lola
Demonstrates Tai Chi

like this:
her right arm rises
slowly   gently

like this:
her fingers unfold
slowly   gently

her fingers fold
her right arm falls
slowly   gently

like this:
her left arm rises
slowly   gently

Adrian Mitchell

like this:
her fingers unfold
slowly   gently

her fingers fold
her left arm falls
slowly   gently

and it is just like walking down
a winding
sandy path
through a mystery garden

just like walking down
to a deep and greeny pool
and seeing
for the first time in your life

a water-lily

All Around the World

Adrian Mitchell

The Wildest Wheelbarrow in the World

It's a Cadillac Subaru Bullnose Lada
With GBH overdrive
It's a Formula Zero
Robert de Niro
The most weed-unfriendly barrow alive
It's got rally-bred CD
Yes indeedy
With a DVD of solid steel
Yes it's the Wildest Wheelbarrow in the World
And it's riding on a wonky wheel

It's the Wildest Wheelbarrow in the World
I never saw another like that
So switch on the telly
And give it some welly
We'll be round the world in eighty seconds flat

It's a woodentop Jaguar Jumback Dolby
With hot and cold data base
It's stereo diesel
Runs like a weasel
With a spookerama smile all over its face

It's got a luxury fountain
A microfiche mountain
With cotton-picking reel-to-reel
Yes it's the Wildest Wheelbarrow in the World
And it's riding on a wonky wheel

It's the Wildest Wheelbarrow in the World
It's proof against bullets and spears
It's chromium-plated
Decaffeinated
And guaranteed for seven thousand years

It's the Wildest Wheelbarrow in the World
I never saw another like that
So switch on the telly
And give it some welly
We'll be round the world in eighty seconds flat

It's the Wildest Wheelbarrow
Wonderfullest Wheelbarrow
Wickedest Wheelbarrow
In the wide wide wide World!

One of the First Poems to be Written Underneath the English Channel or maybe The First

The bones of galleons and their wide-eyed crews,
Haunted by jelly-fish and purple mussels –
They're overhead, stuck in historic ooze –
As our train mumbles through the dark to Brussels.

THE RETURN JOURNEY

As our train mumbles through the dark from Brussels,
They're overhead, stuck in historic ooze –
Haunted by jelly-fish and purple mussels –
The bones of galleons and their wide-eyed crews.

*(This historic poem was written on October 16th 1996 while riding
the Eurostar Train, carriage 16, seat number 76, during the twenty
minutes in which we travelled through the Chunnel. After ten
minutes I realised I could cover the journey home by reversing the
order of the lines. Dedicated to the staff and pupils of the British
School at Brussels.)*

Adrian Mitchell

October

I could eat October
drink its bonfiresmoke
spread my marmalade coloured wings
and walk up the stairs of the sky

I love October leaves
who know better than anyone
how to die happily –
turn pale green
fade to yellow
burn to red
or brown
or gold

then
let go
and
see-saw lightly
down to
where the leaves lie
whispering excitedly
about the bonfire

Blackberry Picking Song

The green little, mean little, lean little berries
Are always at the bottom of the blackberry bush
But the biggest best berries are always high
On the branches way up in the sky.

Though the brambles may scratch
We jump and we hop
For we have to snatch
The ones at the top

Yes, the green little, mean little, lean little berries
Are always at the bottom of the blackberry bush
But the biggest best berries are always high
On the branches way up in the sky.

And those berries we'll cart
Back home to our mam
For blackberry tart
And blackberry jam

For the biggest best berries are always high
On the branches way up in the autumn sky
For blackberry tarts! And blackberry jelly!
And blackberry jam! And wonderful blackberry pie!

Adrian Mitchell

Moondog in New York

There was a man called Moondog
Who made tunes
With thimbles, glasses, zithers,
Keys and spoons
And all the tunes he made
Were living things

Which flew around his head on silver wings

I bought a Moondog record
Fourteen tracks
A red and golden label
Dusty wax
The sounds were delicate
As cowrie shells
The moonlit dancing
Of a thousand bells

313

Umpteen Pockets

My first day in New York
I walked downtown
Moondog sat on the sidewalk
All in brown
He played his instruments
So sweet and wild
I wanted to stay with him
As his child

Adrian Mitchell

Aladdin's Palace

The walls of the Palace are golden
With diamond windows
And ivory doors
Its halls are high
As the sapphire sky
And panthers prowl across
The marble floors

There are courtyards with meadows and rivers
Where hummingbirds hover
And unicorns run
The lofty towers
Stand like shining flowers
And slender minarets
Point to the sun

Umpteen Pockets

An oakwood dinner table five miles long
Laden with silver plates
Of pheasants and salmon
Welsh rabbit and gammon
And pancakes, cherries and chocolate dates
    In the magical Palace

A deep blue swimming pool that's wide and warm
Palm trees and waterslides
And ice cream and peaches
And long surfing beaches
And a dolphin to take you for white-knuckle rides
    Round the magical Palace

Adrian Mitchell

A lake where elephants and hippos swim
And a gorilla tree
Spaniels and foxes
A pool room, juke boxes
And a shopping mall where everything's free –

Down in a studio your favourite band
Plays while you sing along
There are trampolines
All sorts of magic machines
And comical robots which never go wrong
    In the magical Palace

And when you're tired of all this glory
You'll retire to a four-poster bed
Carved angels and dragons
Will sing you a story
Till you dream of the one you'll wed
    In the magical Palace
In the magical Palace of your dreams

Riding West from The Little Bear

I ride a horse called Secrets
A lively dapple-grey
His hoofbeats echo down the trail
They call the Milky Way

Past a stampede of meteors
Down the ravines of space
And over deserts of silver dust
Watchfully we pace

We journey on with hopeful hearts
Though the way's long and far
But sometimes halt and light a fire
Upon some lonesome star

Adrian Mitchell

Moonbathing

All kinds of bathing
Make the body happy
Your mind goes mellow
And your toes turn tappy
Bathing makes your heart bounce like
a rubber ball
But Moonbathing is the best of all

Well I know
Sunbathing is the game to play
Feel your troubles all melting away
Mud bathing's an odd way to wash
But it's fun as you squish and squash

Umpteen Pockets

River bathing is a special treat
If there's no crocodiles after your feet
Honey bathing is sticky but fun
You have to take a steam bath after that one

Yes all kinds of bathing
Make the body happy
Your mind goes mellow
And your toes turn tappy
Bathing makes your heart bounce like
a rubber ball
But Moonbathing is the best of all

Silver beams
Slowly pouring over you
Silver dreams
Are soaring over you
Moon bathing
Dream bathing
Drinking in the light
Of the magical moon
Moonbathing is the best of all!

Adrian Mitchell

In a Japanese City

she is a maker
of tissue paper flowers

gently she bends their petals
pink and blue and ivory
into light blossom patterns

she makes little flowers
they are no bigger than her eyes

approximately roses
approximately daffodils
but never exactly
and sometimes invented flowers
or flowers picked from her
summertime dreamfields

Umpteen Pockets

she makes tissue paper flowers
and scatters them secretly
by ones or by twos
in unexpected places

on a train seat
or a briefcase
on the bonnet of a car
or the brilliant surface of a puddle

she lets drop
one or two
and they drift
towards the ground
and she is out of sight
around the corner
long before they land

Adrian Mitchell

paper kingcups
or buttercups
they sit and wobble
and balance and toboggan
on the small breezes
of the grimy air

she took a basket
of a thousand blossoms
to the top of a tower
in the middle of the city
she emptied them into
a passing cloud and
watched them drift
over streets and schools
and parking lots

a thousand blessings
on the city

Green Dungarees

When I'm invited to a posh party
Or my teacher's dropping round
Or I should be sloshing up
The washing up
I'm never to be found.
And when my uncles start to get hearty
Or I broke a window pane
Or it's time for addition
Or a composition
I've disappeared again –

Adrian Mitchell

I climb into my
Green dungarees
And I put on my
Heavy duty
Garden boots
And I vanish myself
Beyond the trees
And I'm planting shoots
And pulling up roots

And the sun shines down
Like an old yellow cheese
On me at my work
In my green dungarees

Gardening's peaceful when you're on your own
Every now and then you may think a thought
But once in a while I invite a friend
A gardening friend who's not the talkative sort

Umpteen Pockets

We climb into our
Green dungarees
And we put on our
Heavy duty
Garden boots
And we vanish ourselves
Beyond the trees
And we're planting shoots
And pulling up roots

Till the stars shine down
Like bright sweet peas
On me and my friend
In our green dungarees...

Magic Journeys

Who

who invented the moon?
a drop of milk from a porridge-eater's spoon
some ragamuffin from the back of beyond
lifted the lid off a frozen pond
sprinkled it with mashed up mother-of-pearl
and hung it up to stare at the sleepy world
who invented the moon?
some muddlesome young buffoon
stole a princess's silver crown
put it in a cauldron and melted it down
dipped a marble in the molten and soon
out it popped as the moon

who invented the moon?
maybe a rabbit from a TV cartoon
wanted to play soccer with a blonde baboon
they stole some ice cream – vanilla –
from a drowsy old gorilla
and froze it round a blue balloon
and there was the moon
there was the moon
there was the dear old moon

A Lost Princess

In the rusty murk
In the musty dark
A long boat slides
Along the lake

And at its prow
Stands the Lost Princess
With moondust scattered
On her midnight balldress

Through a battered brass telescope
The Sad Pirate watches her disappear
And his face turns into a marble rock
And his heart to a starry tear

The Mucky Princess

The mucky Princess
liked to play in the mud
she would wallow and roll and dig

The mucky Princess
loved the mud so much
she found a new job as a pig.

A Surprise Parcel

Hairy green string
Blobs of purple sealing-wax
Six postage stamps bearing silver holograms
Of the Snow Queen on an iceberg throne
Muddy brown wrapping paper
Round a soggy heavy cardboard box
When you sway it from side to side
You hear a swishing-swashing sound

Somebody has sent you a river

The Quest of the
Deep-Freeze Knight

My armour is wafers
My helmet's a cone
As I fearlessly march
Through the Ice-cream Zone

I journey on
Towards my duty
Through the bright Forest
Of Tutti Frutti

Past Strawberry Hill
And Vanilla-Tree
I keep my mind chill
And military

Adrian Mitchell

Then under a bush
Of Pistachios
I trim my ferocious
Moustachios

Then I don silver boots
And onwards I trudge
Over the Desert
Of Chocolate Fudge

Will I see
From some far and fatal ridge –
Cassata Castle
And the King of the Fridge?

Hampstead Heath Haiku

Kites in summertime

Toboggans in wintertime

Dogs all the year round

Adrian Mitchell

My Lost Dog

You were lost in my dream
I was looking for you everywhere
Somebody told me to try the station
It looked like you on the railway bridge

The railwaymen had turned their signal box
Into a wooden restaurant
They cooked in bright red buckets which said FIRE
But the inside of their buckets were polished gold

You were lost in my dream
I was looking for you anywhere
I was just going to cry when I woke up –
      And here you are

Secret Country

(from The Pied Piper*)*

There is no money
So there's no crime
There are no watches
'Cos there's no time
It's a good country
It's a secret country
And it's your country and mine

If something's needed
You make it there
And we have plenty
For we all share
It's a kind country
It's a secret country
And it's your country and mine

There are no cages
There is no zoo
But the free creatures
Come and walk with you
It's a strange country

Adrian Mitchell

It's a secret country
And it's your country and mine

There are no prisons
There are no poor
There are no weapons
There is no war
It's a safe country
It's a secret country
And it's your country and mine

And in that country
Grows a great tree
And it's called Freedom
And its fruit is free
In that blue country
In that warm country
In that loving country
In that wild country

In that secret country
Which is your country and mine

Daft as a Doughnut

Adrian Mitchell

Some Sad Story

I am Fred
My head
Is made of bread

I lay down
Beside a pond
Along come
A quacker and a swan

Hey!
Where's my bread head gone?

CRUMBS!!!

Good Old Mud

Poets and mud
Attract each other
For poets know
Mud was our Mother.

Great things are done
When mud and poets meet
But nothing good is done
In Oxford Street.

Adrian Mitchell

I Saw Two Ghosts

I saw two ghosts when I was six
Two ghosts in one night

The first ghost was a small squat woman
Almost a cube shape
Head like a squashed box
Her mouth a dark pillarbox slot

And then I slept

The second ghost came when I woke again
Standing where the woman had stood
The second ghost was a big square butcher
Holding a huge mallet
Looking both pleased and savage
Obviously the man who flattened Little Boxhead

Umpteen Pockets

But when daylight came
I saw the two of them
Reduced to a wooden wardrobe
With luggage stacked beside it

My terror laughed itself away

Nowadays I'm not scared of ghosts
But I'm terrified of wardrobes

Adrian Mitchell

The Giant's Love Song

Oh my love's enormous, just like me,
And just like me, she's true
And her eyes are like two basketballs
If basketballs were blue.

When my darling whispers in my ear
It is like a blunderbuss
And my love is dainty to be seen
As St Pancras Terminus.

Oh her face is like the scarlet sun
When the tropical sunset falls
And her breast is like Mount Everest
And her dome is like St Paul's.

Umpteen Pockets

Yes, her hair is like a forest fire,
Like a glowing tower her nose
And her teeth stand in her mighty gums
Like tombstones in two rows.

Her knees are like two pyramids
When she's lying very still
And her foot is like a river barge
And her bottom's like Primrose Hill.

Oh my love's at least one hundred times
As big and fair as you.
Yes, my love's enormous, just like me.
And just like me, she's true.

Backhead

This morning I woke up with a grunt
To find my head was on back to front

A Warning to Those who Fly

If you break wind in outer space
The gas that you expel
May freeze into a solid mass –
A planet made of smell

And living creatures may evolve
To praise with all their heart
The great creator of their home,
The fragrant Planet Fart.

Adrian Mitchell

Ancestor Maths

You were born from
    two parents
and four grandparents
who were born from your
    eight great-grandparents
who came from your
    sixteen great-great-grandparents
who were produced by your
    thirty-two great-great-great grandparents
about 240 years ago.
Now they came from your
    sixty-four great-great-great-great grandparents
who were born to your
    128 great-great-great-great-great grandparents
who issued from your
    265 great-great-great-great-great-great
grandparents descended from your
    512 great-great-great-great-great-great-great
      grandparents
        around 540 years ago.

Umpteen Pockets

But they didn't come from nowhere they came
    from your
      1,024 great-great-great-great-great-great-great-great
          grandparents
            who sprang from your
    2,048 great-great-great-great-great-great-great-great-great
          grandparents
            who were the children of your
    4,096 great-great-great-great-great-great-great-great-great-
          great grandparents
            who were created by your
    8,192 great-great-great-great-great-great-great-great-great-
          great-great grandparents
            say 720 years ago.

Well, they must be the offspring of your
    16,384 great x12 grandparents
born to your
    32,768 great x 13 grandparents
made by your
    65,536 great x 14 grandparents
produced by your
    131,072 great x 15 grandparents
    who thrived about a thousand years ago –
        say 1,000 AD approximately.
So their mothers and fathers were your
    262,144 great x 16 grandparents
spawned by your
    524,288 great x 17 grandparents
who must be the children of your
    1,048,576 great x 18 grandparents
born and raised by your
    2,097,152 great x 19 grandparents
maybe one thousand two hundred and forty
        years ago.

To cut a long story shortish you had
4,194,304 great x 20 grandparents,
8,388,608 great x 21 grandparents,
16,777,216 great x 22 grandparents
33,554,432 great x 23 grandparents
67,108,864 great x 24 grandparents
134,217,728 great x 25 grandparents
268,435,456 great x 26 grandparents

like, 1,640 years ago.

And – you had
536,870,912 great x 27 grandparents
1,073,741,824 great x 28 grandparents
2,147,483,648 great x 29 grandparents
4,294,967,296 great x 30 grandparents
8,589,934,592 great x 31 grandparents
17,179,869,184 great x 32 grandparents

exactly two thousand years ago...

hey!

Adrian Mitchell

just a minute!
hangaboutabit!
Two thousand years ago the population of
  the world
    was only 200 million people.
But you had 17 billion, 179 million,
    869 thousand 1884
        super-great grandparents hanging around at
      the time.

Doesn't add up.

We have a problem.

17,179,869,184 minus 2,000,000
      seems to me to equal
16,979,869,184 grandparents
      who just weren't there.
Seems to me that 16,979,869,184 of
            your incredibly great grandparents –

MUST HAVE
COME FROM
OUTER SPACE!

Adrian Mitchell

Wrong Planet Blues

Born on the wrong planet
But I do the best I can
This is not my planet
But I do the best I can
Wake up early every morning
Disguise myself as a man

Go out and earn a living
Just like human beings do
Scrape some kind of living
Just like human beings do
Watch me acting the part of a Person
In the Human Being Zoo

Umpteen Pockets

Born on the wrong planet
But I'll be going home some day
This is not my planet
I'll go home some sweet day
The skeleton rocketship
Coming to fly me away

Back to my homeland
Back where I belong
Back to my own planet
Singing a cheerful song
Back to a planet that feels right to me
Even when I'm doing wrong

Adrian Mitchell

On my Rooftop

bounding
resounding
a massive stream
a shuddering
flood
surrounded by steam

too warm to be snow
too wild to be rain
it must be that weak-bladdered
Giant again
that ogre in a toga
that gynormous goof –

PIDDLER ON THE ROOF!

What's a Basin?

A basin means
You have a hot lake when you want one
And a cold lake when you want one –
A lake big enough
For your hands to go swimming in.

When your hands are tired of swimming
Take them out and shake them.
Your hands make rain.
Then you yank out the plug

And gravity chases
The lake down a spiral fun ride
To vanish
Like an otter into a riverbank.

Twenty-one Secrets of Poetry

(Every art and craft and sport and skill has its Secrets. Here are some of the Secrets I've learned which may help you write your own poems)

One
Use your feet
To find the beat

Two
If the old word won't do
Make up a new

Three
Don't write about Autumn
'Cos that's the season –
Write your poems
For a real reason

Four
Write to cool down
Write to get hot
Write about things
You like a lot

Adrian Mitchell

Five
Write for other people;
Quite a few
Will sit down and write
A poem for you

Six
Like a poppy-field poppy
Be happy to copy

Seven
Good ideas often fly off, and so
Take that notebook wherever you go
  (and three pens)

Eight
You can rhyme every time at the end of a line
And that's no crime if the words feel fine,
But on the other hand you can write a poem
Which doesn't have any rhymes at all

Nine
What can you write about?
It helps very much
If you choose something
You can see and touch

Ten
Maybe the search for food,
Maybe a quest for glory,
But write a poem
Which tells a story

Eleven
Pile up your feelings
On a poetry plate –
Write about something
You really hate

Twelve
To make a poem
That lasts a minute
Daydream for hours
Before you begin it

Thirteen

Don't just write
For the literate few –
Write for babies
And animals too

Fourteen

When you read to a friend
Or recite to a crowd
Say your poem
Slow and loud

Fifteen

Poetry's a lovely, dangerous game
But it's very unlikely to bring you fame
So don't try to live by your poetry
You'd earn more selling cat food on Mercury

Sixteen

Sad poems, funny poems –
Feel everything you're writing.
Rough poems, gentle poems –
Make them all exciting

Seventeen

It's pretty tiring
Just being you –
Write from other people's
Points of view
Use lots of different voices and you may
End up with a poem
That becomes a play

Eighteen

All you can do with
 your life
Is live it
Poetry's a gift –
So give it

Nineteen

If you want to learn
How to talk to grass
Or dance the giraffe
Or imitate glass
Invite a poet
Into your class

Twenty

Write a secret poem
That you never show
Learn it and burn it
So nobody will know

Twenty-One

These are Secrets.
None of them are Rules
Here's another Secret:
There are no Rules in poetry

(Except the ones you make up for yourself
Which you can break whenever you like.)

Words for a Springtime Poem

adoring

adorning

alarming

alerting

charming

charring

chirruping

churning

coursing

courting

dairying

dallying

exerting

emerging

ferrying

flirting

glorying
glowing
harrying
hurrying

marrying
mourning

piercing

querying

shirting
skirting
slurring
slurping
smarting
smirking
snarling
snorting
sparking
sparring
sporting
spurning
spurring
spurting

starling
starring
starting
starving
sterling
stirring
storming

swarming

swerving
swirling
tarrying
twirling
wearying
whirling
yearling
yearning
zpring!

Adrian Mitchell

Writer Wriddles

The Tale of Eat A Rabbit by Beatrix Rotter

The Tale of Jemima Crispyduck by Beatrix Hotter

Harry Potter and the Tenpins of Fire by J K Bowling

The Adventures of Huckleberry Hound by Bark Twain

Robinson Floppyears by Spaniel Defoe

The Sowman by Raymond Piggs

Charlie and the Curry Factory by Tarka Dal

Sticky Island by Robert Gluey Stevenson

Alice in Beerland by Lewis Barrel

The Merchant of Jelly by William Shakespoon

The Tragedy of Macbeef by William Steakspeare

The Loaftrap by Agatha Crusty

Phoney-O and Juliet by William Fakespeare

Big Fat Dorrit by Charles Thickens

Bleak Coop by Charles Chickens

The Merchant of Tennis by Wimbledon Shakespeare

A Midsummer Night's Insomnia by William Wakespeare

The Canterbury Cups by Geoffrey Saucer

Paradise Cheese by John Stilton

The Song of Lowerwatha by Shortfellow

Body in Toytown by Enid Frighten

Animal Hospital by George Unwell

The Illustrated Bum by Jacqueline Wilmoon

The Lunchpack of Notre Dame by Pizza Tugo

The Big Spot of the Baskervilles by Arthur Conan Boil

The Ghoul and the Vampirebat Went To Sea by Edward Fear

Adrian Mitchell

Is this a Poem or a Doughnut?

When is a Poem a Doughnut,
Asks the ancient riddle?
When it can roll and it has a big hole
Or a blob of red jam in the middle.

You may say mine are as fresh as a daisy
Or dry as a dinosaur bone,
But if you don't fancy my doughnuts like crazy –
Bake your own!

Index of First Lines

The End